SEASONAL MATTERS RURAL RELATIONS
(Field)notes on rhythms, rituals and cohabitation
By Seasonal Neighbours

I0110012

Seasonal
Matters
Rural
Relations

How long is the journey?

> A finished bathroom, a renovated
> home, a space to rest in old age
> or host the children when they visit.

How long is the journey?

> 1000 euros, 5000 euros, a one-
> storey house that stands a
> little taller than the neighbours'.

How long is the journey?

> A place to rest, where your
> mental health, gender and beliefs
> are not a mishap.

How long is the journey?

> Until the children start school,
> finish school, or no longer share
> the house they grew up in.

How long is the journey?

TABLE OF CONTENT

Prologue

EDITORIAL

The agricultural hinterlands of Western Europe provide the urban food supply. An unbalanced urban-rural relationship has fostered the ever-increasing industrialization and automation of agriculture and the transformation of farming practices and labour. Even traditional relationships, between humans and non-humans, plants, the weather and the rhythm of the seasons, are being lost in the race for profit and for increasingly intensive methods of production. More and more, crops are grown year-round in sterile, air-conditioned environments, losing the connection with seasons, with the soil, with the rain and sun.

The free flow of labour in the EU has created a new dynamic in the countryside, with an ever-growing and ever-diversifying group of temporary workers following harvests. This impacts both their homelands and the countries of arrival.

As an interdisciplinary collective, Seasonal Neighbours attempts to observe, record and archive narratives for the existing, disappearing and newly emerging relationships in the countryside and to understand what role our artistic practices can play in this process.

By immersing ourselves in fieldwork in a variety of farms, greenhouses and villages across Western Europe, we engaged in the practice of neighbouring, spending time working alongside temporary agricultural workers, learning from them, inhabiting landscapes together with other entities that are often absent in the agricultural narrative such as insects and plants.

The rural realities we encountered are foreign to most consumers. In mainstream culture, the future of the countryside is often presented through flat images of vast uniform fields and greenhouses with little human presence, on the one hand, and densely populated metropolises, on the other. Considering capitalist market dynamics and the environmental premise, this situation looks, as philosopher and architecture theorist Sébastien Marot argues, both inevitable and impossible.

We want to complexify this image by depicting this reality in its multidimensional nature as a diverse landscape with many different shades, voices and relationships. We highlight the different sensibilities connected to them to take the first steps towards rethinking the countryside.

This book gathers the different nuances of the agricultural realities experienced by the collective members in our neighbouring processes, shaping a variety of contributions from visual essays to graphic collages, poems, maps, short stories, picking songs and musical scores to recipes using weeds.

Additionally, we interviewed carefully selected experts who shared their vision and gave our experiences a theoretical framework. Trade unionist Arnd Spahn talks about the realities of mobile work today and how national and international regulations affect its social and legal position. Carolien Lubberhuizen shares her anthropological research on the arrival routines of migrant workers in agricultural contexts in Belgium and the Netherlands. With Fernando García-Dory (Inland), we held a conversation about long-term forms of artistic engagement with rural contexts. And Sébastien Marot provides his perspective on how seasonal work fits into four different scenarios on the future of architecture and agriculture that he developed.

Members of the collective also reflected on our process and some of the common topics within Seasonal Neighbours: Ewoud Vermote shares his reflections on the critical and political questions about representation and the ethical positioning that Seasonal Neighbours faced during the collective artistic endeavour, while Anastasia Eggers discusses how our artistic interventions relate to new forms of seasonality (and post-seasonality) and theories of rural rituals.

After bringing together all the contributions in this book we come to ask ourselves again:
How long is the journey?

TWO WEEKS IN HOOGSTRATEN
BY MAX

>7h
Pick Cut Shower Cut Cut Shower Cut
>9h (others stayed longer)
Cut Shower Cut (cut myself) Put sprayer into
plants Cut Shower Pot Cut Freeze
>9,5h (others stayed longer)
Hang plants right Cut Put sprayer into plants
Harvest Pot
>9,5h (others stayed longer)
Harvest Cut Pot Cut Harvest
>6h (teaching in the morning)
Cut Harvest Cut Shower Harvest

(others worked)
(day off)

>10h (tried to prove myself)
Harvest Plant Plant Plant Place pots on heels
Harvest
>10,5h (tried to prove myself)
Harvest Cut Shower Plant Cut Cut Shower Cut
>9h (others stayed longer)
Harvest Cut Shower Cut Cut Shower Plant Cut
>10,5h (tried to prove myself)
Harvest Place pots on heels Cut Shower Harvest
Plant Empty greenhouse
>9h (others stayed longer)
Cut Harvest Empty greenhouse Cut Shower Cut
Install greenhouse

THE ARTIST AS VISITOR

Ethics and Politics of Seasonal Neighbours

Ewoud Vermote

Seasonal Neighbours emerged from a project call for artists, writers, designers and researchers to artistically explore the theme of seasonal labour from a personal work experience in the agricultural sector. The first part of the collective artistic research involved fieldwork: picking pears or strawberries, working on a farm, packaging vegetables. The goal of the project was to allow artists to embed and immerse themselves in the real-life context of seasonal work, to develop an artistic project that would be presented locally in the fields, and to create a collective exhibition project in a major art institute in Belgium.

Already at the first collective meeting aimed at processing the fieldwork experiences, a number of critical and political questions concerning representation, ethical positioning and power structures emerged in the group: How to speak 'with' instead of 'about'? How to avoid portraying the hyper-diverse group of seasonal workers as a homogeneous whole? How not to impose narratives of victimization or, conversely, represent the farmers who contract seasonal workers as mere evildoers? Many of the conversations circled around these unresolved issues of representing an unknown other in socially engaged art practices.

Ewoud Vermote took part in the collective research as a writer and critical thinker. In this article he reflects on the ethical and political questions raised by the members during the process.

CREATING DISTANCE:
THE ARTIST AS VISITOR

Although each of the fourteen participating artists followed their own practice and methodology, common threads quickly emerged across the various projects. They all tended to focus on the global rather than the personal, the plural rather than the singular, and each project entered into dialogue with the work, the workers, the field, the crops rather than withdrawing into personal reflection.

It is striking how none of the creative processes of the artists addressed the most obvious: the suffering of separated families, the harsh working conditions, the exploitation and social abuses around cheap labour that occasionally make the news... While dealing with a difficult social and political issue like seasonal labour, the artists deliberately avoided taking the position of the 'empathetic outsider' which Susan Sontag so conscientiously addresses in her essay *Regarding the Pain of Others*: "So far as we feel sympathy, we feel we are not accomplices to what caused the suffering. Our sympathy proclaims our innocence as well as our impotence."[1] Without questioning your own involvement in suffering and structures of inequality, the conditions that make these structures possible become perpetuated. Although perhaps unintended, privileged persons speaking for less privileged

1   Susan Sontag, *Regarding the Pain of Others* (New York: Penguin, 2004), 102.

groups often reinforce and affirm existing hierarchies. So as an artist you have to be aware of the position you are speaking from. Linda Alcoff makes this painstakingly clear in her text *The Problem of Speaking for Others*[2] where she writes that where one speaks from influences the truth, meaning and consequences of what one says. Every representation is always mediated and a product of interpretation, which gives quite some power to the one who is representing. Being very conscious and aware of this dynamic and their own positionality in this project, the members of Seasonal Neighbours chose for a methodological and ethical backbone based on dialogue, understanding and pluralism.

In their essay *Encountering the Stranger: Hannah Arendt and the Shortcomings of Empathy as a Moral Compass,* Noomi Matthiesen and Jacob Klitmøller use the writings of Arendt to explore this further. They argue (via Arendt) that the position of the empathic outsider is based on a thought process that produces sameness, closing the space of difference and understanding. Therefore, rather than putting ourselves in the perspective of the other, Arendt advocates a gesture of visiting: not the appropriation of the other's perspective, but the examination of the world from that other's perspective, taking into account their specific sociopolitical

2   Linda Alcoff, "The Problem of Speaking for Others", *Cultural Critique* 20 (1991): 5–32, https://doi.org/10.2307/1354221.

Prologue

conditions and position.[3] Matthiesen and Klitmøller describe it as follows: "Worldliness, understanding the world from multiple perspectives, thus supersedes empathy, which merely calls for experiencing the world from the perspective of a single other by looking inward and reflecting on one's own experience."[4] It is neither by looking into ourselves nor by looking into another that understanding becomes possible, but through our ability to look out into the world from the perspective of another. In other words, understanding is never a simple act of discovery but a never-ending dialogue with the pluralities that our world abounds in and the critical reflection this incites.

The work of German artist and filmmaker Harun Farocki exemplifies how this can translate into a socially engaged artistic practice. Farocki advocated a form of empathy that instead of compassion produces an effect of alienation, hereby critically opening up to the world in which the individual is enmeshed and making the recipient think about their place in the world.[5] For example, his video installation *In Comparison* (2009) relates different techniques in brickmaking and how these techniques create space, organize social relationships

3   Noomi Matthiesen and Jacob Klitmøller, "Encountering the Stranger: Hannah Arendt and the Shortcomings of Empathy as a Moral Compass", *Theory & Psychology* 29, no. 2 (2019): 182–99, https://doi.org/10.1177/0959354319828174.

4   Matthiesen and Klitmøller, "Encountering the Stranger", 193.

5   Harun Farocki, "Empathy", in *Harun Farocki: Another Kind of Empathy*, eds. Carles Guerra and Antje Ehmann (London: Koenig, 2007), 105.

and store knowledge about social structures. The installation observes and untangles these different relationships without appropriating a single perspective: each brick, in any culture, comes into contact with toiling hands; each machine squeaks, rolls and turns. No voice-over, no interviews, no testimonials. The work departs from the concrete matter of brickmaking and the world it is enveloped in – languidly laughing with colleagues, in the solitude of an automated factory hall, rushing and buckling in the mud. Instead of focusing on a particular aspect of brick-making, it connects technique, material, process, industrial production and labour conditions, movements and gestures, etc. into a complex interconnected whole. *In Comparison* shows what its title implies: all these modes of brickmaking are part of the same world, they exist next to each other and every technique speaks not only about itself, but also gives meaning to the cultures that brought forth other techniques. By exploring it as a cultural phenomenon, it becomes a method of exploring and understanding the world in its full plurality.

SEASONAL LABOUR AS A CULTURAL PHENOMENON

In order to create a work of art, the members of Seasonal Neighbours had to find ways to distance themselves from their personal picking experiences. The harsh conditions of the fieldwork created intimate connections with fellow seasonal workers,

The Artist as Visitor

farmers and local residents, moments of misery and laughter were shared, and temporary friendships were forged. Some were witness to blatant racism and discrimination, others saw how their colleagues enjoyed great prestige in their local communities through seasonal labour. Engaging in personal and intimate relationships that occurred during the fieldwork made some of the artists struggle with their own position, feeling like a privileged observer, an outsider, an impostor.

Trying to avoid the position of sympathetic outsider, the artists sought to transcend individual, emotional and ethical conflicts that surround seasonal labour and the personal stories of social injustice they encountered. Instead, they started drawing wider circles that explore the complex and multilayered world that structures and produces current forms of seasonal labour. Based on their own background and research interests, the artists looked at the topic from a perspective of interconnectedness, of global and local food production and consumption, through the relations between plants, hands and automated machines, between a highly volatile market economy and traditional views on rural life, the brutal disconnect between automated greenhouses and natural forms of seasonality, and reflected on the importance of rural heritage, rituals and symbolism, housing and architecture, the complexities of living in a multilingual setting of temporary habitation.

Rather than diving into personal testimonies (gazing into the other) or interpreting what they saw by connecting it to personal histories or experiences (gazing into the self), they thought about how they could look at the world, understand it, by exploring seasonal labour as a broader and multifaceted cultural phenomenon. In doing this, they entered into dialogue with a multitude of actors: workers, farmers, inhabitants, family members, architects, etc. These encounters became an opportunity to recognize the world in all its complexity and plurality and to experience the interconnectedness of ideological, historical, social, economic and individual elements that enter into play.

Let's look at a few examples. The architectural research of Ciel Grommen and Maximiliaan Royakkers explored the complex interrelations that arise between cultures and nations and how the exchange of workers directly impacts residential typologies in the homeland of Romanian workers. Their work examined more closely how seasonal labour not only creates upward social mobility, but moreover how Western architectural styles and the associated lifestyles they represent are adopted by the workers, affecting the aesthetic and social fabric of their home countries. Although in a different style, the project resonated with that of Ioana Lupascu, who developed the audio walk *I'm looking at her looking at them looking at me*. The sound piece engages in a personal reflection on how stories of seasonal work abroad give shape to the landscape, architec-

Prologue

ture, habits, food and conversations in the Romanian village of Ioana's childhood summers. A different story of international circulation of people and goods was explored in *Sending Roots: Witloof in Transit*. For her project, Pia Jacques wanted to send a single chicory to Thailand as a simple gesture of friendship between two former colleagues in a chicory farm. It became a Kafkaesque administrative process reflecting on the impact of border regulations where the mobility of vegetables is far more restricted and monitored by international law than that of human workers.

In drawing out the complex worldliness of seasonal labour, other artists were drawn to the more-than-human relationships that surround the agricultural work seasonal labourers are involved in. How is the care of plants, insects, the changing of seasons involved in the worldliness of seasonal labour? And how is it articulated in an industry that is driven forward by increasing mechanization and upscaling, where food production is increasingly cut loose from seasons, the sun and natural growth patterns? Indeed, these questions are just as much part of the worldliness around seasonal labour, where the social and the natural, economy and ecology can't be thought of separately. The dichotomy between self and environment – not as something we live with, but as something that can/should always be controlled and shaped – is a false one. The growth of a plant, the buzzing of a bee, is never without meaning. It is intimately connected to each of us, to the food we eat, to the hands of the worker. By focusing on the plants, Seasonal Neighbours does not render invisible the workers; instead it draws ever-wider circles from the workers and the field to the broader cultural ideologies, how seasonal labour is set in the way we think of food, plants, growth, seasons and the economy.

THE UNINVITED VISITOR

After their fieldwork experience, each artist was invited to develop an in situ work. The collective's goal was to bring the research back to the contexts they worked in to present the questions to the people involved and evoke a new kind of dialogue through an artistic intervention. This resulted in a diversity of projects: temporary installations, informal cooking sessions, a ritualistic procession, a concert in a strawberry greenhouse, conversations, and more.

Let's take a closer look at the local radio shows developed by artist Mona Thijs. After her fieldwork experience, Mona decided to revisit several fruit farms of the region with a mobile radio studio. Together with a Bulgarian and a Polish interpreter, she asked the seasonal workers what music was meaningful to them while working here in Belgium. Behind the music, a field of stories and meanings emerged, which Mona processed into new narratives that took the form of radio shows. In it she mixed songs picked by workers with reflections on multilingualism and the political potential of music. The shows, entitled, *Playlist van de Pluk,* were broadcast on a local station, Radio VRW.

By focusing on multilingualism and music, Mona, like the other members of the collective, chose to approach seasonal labour as a cultural phenomenon. The audience Mona reached was twofold. First there is the hyperlocal context of the farm. With her mobile radio station and music installation, Mona performed her role as interviewer for an audience of seasonal labourers and farmers. A second audience was reached via the radio shows that were broadcast locally. Addressing these two audiences, Mona manoeuvred a series of ethical questions. She first made sure the form and aesthetics were comprehensible for the audience present at the farm: workers, inhabitants and passers-by. As an interpreter was present, the workers could speak in their own language, addressing Mona as well as their colleagues. In the final radio shows, Mona used accessible language, without being didactic. Secondly, as she worked directly with the names, stories and voices of people, she had to resist instrumentalization. Mona's project steered clear from this trap by establishing a relationship of reciprocity with her audience. She collected their stories and in exchange played music, offering a moment of play and shared laughs. Roles of speaking and listening were shifted. This produced a kind of 'dialogical pedagogy' that goes against what radical pedagogue Paulo Freire calls the 'banking'

The Artist as Visitor

concept of education: knowledge as a gift to passive receivers who are considered to know nothing. Instead, it realizes that 'everyone knows things they have learned in their relations with the world and with other humans'.[6] The implications are real: the workers become subjects who are listened to, who know instead of who are being known about. By focusing on language and music, Mona avoids a space of sad stories, victimization and consumptive identification. She is not an expert in the topics talked about, nor are they; both enter into a shaky dialogue, a conversation rather than a representation of any kind of truth or true identity. The goal is mutual: to come to an understanding of each other.

By choosing a local radio station, she stayed true to her engagement: giving a voice to those who are invisible. Not in a museum or on a popular podcast, which would contribute to the visibility of Mona as an artist, but in the context where the stories were collected. Inhabitants who tuned in listened to their invisible co-inhabitants, as such creating a space for precisely the kind of 'visiting' that Hannah Arendt speaks about, making you receptive to different voices, opinions and values. As the radio show revolves around the farms of the workers, just around the corner from where the listeners of Radio VRW live, the symbolic, poetic and ambiguous nature of these shows kept a strong link with

6   Paulo Freire, *Pedagogy of the Oppressed* (London: Penguin, 2017), 37.

the concrete. Although editorial control and authorship remained with Mona, the project shows the strength of 'speaking with' instead of 'speaking for'.

THE ARTIST IN THE MUSEUM: OUR INVISIBLE HANDS

After the in situ interventions, the artist collective started working on the group exhibition *Our Invisible Hands.* This took place in collaboration with the internationally acclaimed arts centre Z33 House for Contemporary Art, Design and Architecture in Hasselt, a provincial Flemish town near the agricultural region Haspengouw.

The scenography of the exhibition was organized in four rooms. The first was the entrance hall that featured residues of in situ interventions or projects whose primary existence was elsewhere. In room 1, three projects were gathered under the name 'Temporary Neighbours'. These interacted with the relations that farmers, local workers and inhabitants have with seasonal labourers. Room 2, 'Here and There', gathered the projects that spoke about how it feels to live in two places, personal memories, etc. The final room 'Human Beings and Crops' presented projects that dealt with the notion of multispecies cohabitation. Various activities took place over the course of the exhibition: a dance performance during the vernissage, a ritualistic procession which took off from the arts centre into

31   Prologue

the fields, as well as cooking sessions, and conversations with invited stakeholders.

The position of the artists as temporary visitors, fieldworkers who enter into dialogue with a specific context, was unsettled when they traded this moment of interaction and dialogue for an institutional artistic context. The carefully constructed network of connections and perspectives elaborated during the artist's fieldwork and the resulting interventions in the field had to be translated into the format of an artwork that speaks to an institutional audience of artists, art lovers and art critics.

The careful positioning of the artists was translated by others, the institute and its mediation, the press, towards the museum visitors. Scenographically, this took the form of three white spaces and a darkened space for the video installations. The background information about the various projects was kept to a minimum: one A4 covered the eleven projects. For more details, the public was redirected to the website of Seasonal Neighbours. In the press, some of the reviews ran headlines like 'Artists Become Seasonal Workers', as if seasonal work was only interesting now that it was being presented by artists that worked as temporary fieldworkers, now that it was being presented as symbolic artworks in an art institute, instead of through the direct message of an activist or the testimony of workers.

The artistic freedom and the distance created by circling around the core social issues, the divergent links and connections to the worlds that constitute seasonal labour (physical, global, artificial, seasonal, natural, economic) left certain visitors puzzled and confused, sometimes even disappointed or angry. The decision not to portray the workers directly was interpreted by some as perpetuating the invisibility of the seasonal worker, going directly against the audience's expectation of making the invisible hands visible. The playfulness of some of the projects and the focus on the more-than-human was seen by some critical viewers as an affront to the structural inequality underlying seasonal labour.

To some of the artists, it felt like their careful entangling of the larger contexts around seasonal work was lost in translation and that their attempt to produce an alternative form of attention to the issue was seen as replacing rather than complementing other forms of attention as they intended. This was in sharp contrast to the enthusiasm expressed for the local small-scale interventions like the *Sacred Fire Pot Procession* that took place in the fields or the local radio broadcasts of Mona Thijs. As Nato Thompson argues in his essay *Ethical Considerations in Public Art,* the questions 'Is this art?' and 'Which frame of reference do I need to use here?' are of no importance in those public contexts.[7] Instead,

---

7   Nato Thompson, "Ethical Considerations in Public Art," *Scandalous*, ed. Nina Möntmann (London: Sternberg Press, 2013), 106–23.

they can be replaced by the question, 'What is this and why does this deserve my attention?' In those site-specific projects, the symbolic translations of seasonal labour into works of art were always connected to the concrete reality of the field. Mona's radio shows, which reflected on multilingualism, were recorded at local farms in conversation with the workers. This opened up a generous environment for the listeners to interpret this artwork according to a chosen frame of reference.

However, in the museum, Mona didn't renegotiate this position, adapting it instead to the institutional context. The radio shows and their local audiences were re-enacted through a small installation with garden furniture and a radio, combined with an A4 with a QR code and some information about the project. The installation merely documented the in situ intervention. For the visitors who scanned the QR code and listened to the shows, it was harder to defend against instrumentalization: they didn't necessarily live in the local context, they didn't have to question their role in this framework, there was no position of discomfort. Its strength was clearly the actual intervention.

Where an in situ intervention leaves a lot of space for the public to enter into an active dialogue with what they see, according to their own frames of reference, the traditional institutional context of the art world tends to leave less room for that. The context isn't given. So what ways could we imagine to make the concrete, tangible reality of the field more present during the exhibition? Workshops and round-table conversations are dialogical tools that serve this goal, although only for the participants. One particular example comes to mind. In the dance performance *Nomadics*, Lisbeth Gruwez and Maarten Van Cauwenberghe explore the relation between body and landscape. The performance was held in a typical black box theatre; however, before seeing the actual play, the audience and performers walked together from the countryside to the city. After that, they entered the theatre with a shared experience, taking it along through the performance.

I imagine the audience of the Seasonal Neighbours exhibition first going on this walk: through the fields, along the orchards that extend for kilometres, pointing out the discreet sleeping facilities, the trucks that ride on and off, talking about what they see before arriving at the exhibition with new eyes. It would be an exciting experiment that would definitely raise interesting new questions: Who is guiding and who is following? Who is speaking and who is listening? Who decides what information gets shared? From which position do we enter the field then? Curious, observing, privileged again?

RHYTHMS OF THE FIELDS

Mapping the Work

Claire Chassot, Anastasia Eggers,
Maximiliaan Royakkers

Ines listened to strawberries at work in a greenhouse in Hoogstraten (Belgium).

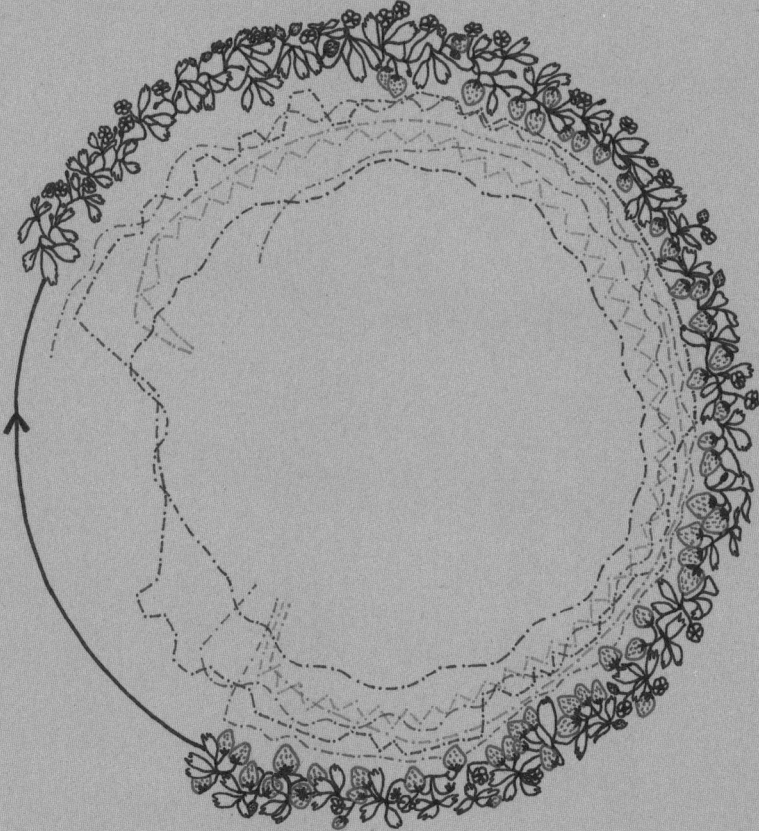

Prologue

Ciel and Maximiliaan worked in a strawberry greenhouse in Hoogstraten (Belgium) with Romanian families and afterwards visited their homes.

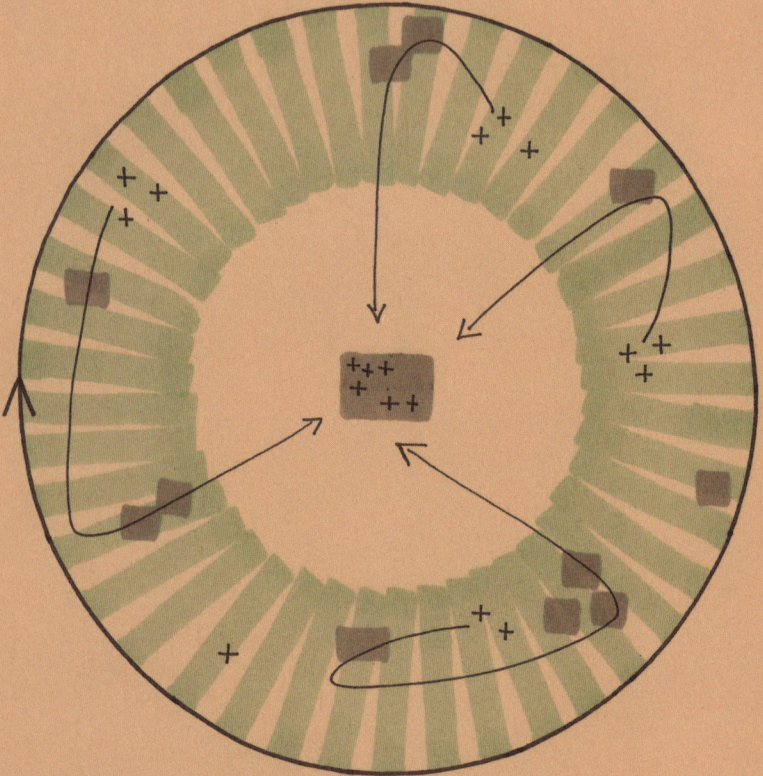

Rhythms of the Fields

Jonathan worked in a pear orchard in Belgium alongside
Polish workers and later visited their region of origin.

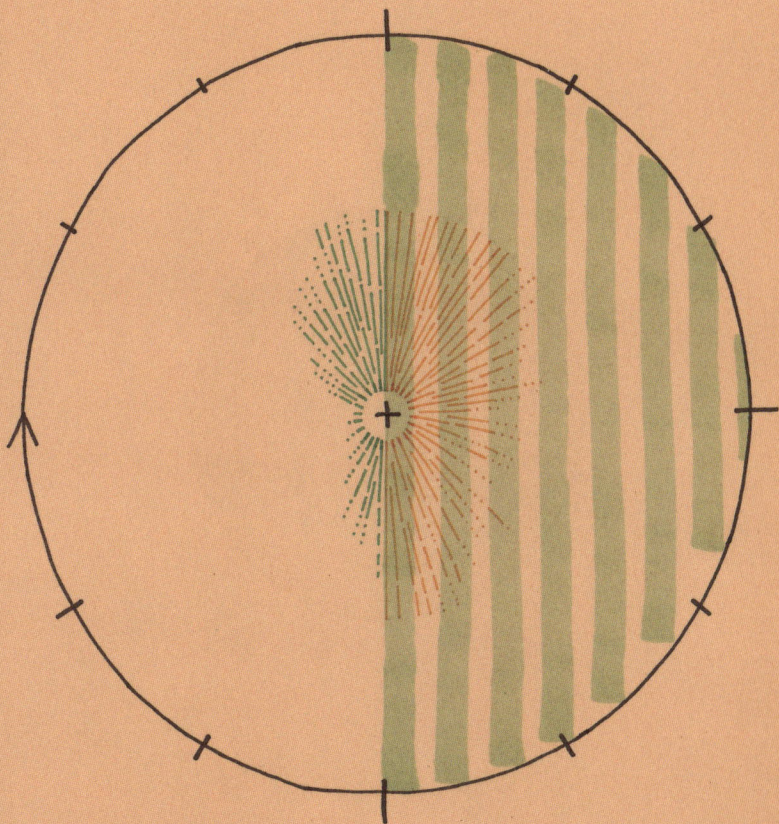

Prologue

Pia worked in a *witloofkot*, the packaging line of a chicory farm in
Kampenhout (Belgium), alongside Belgian and Thai female workers.

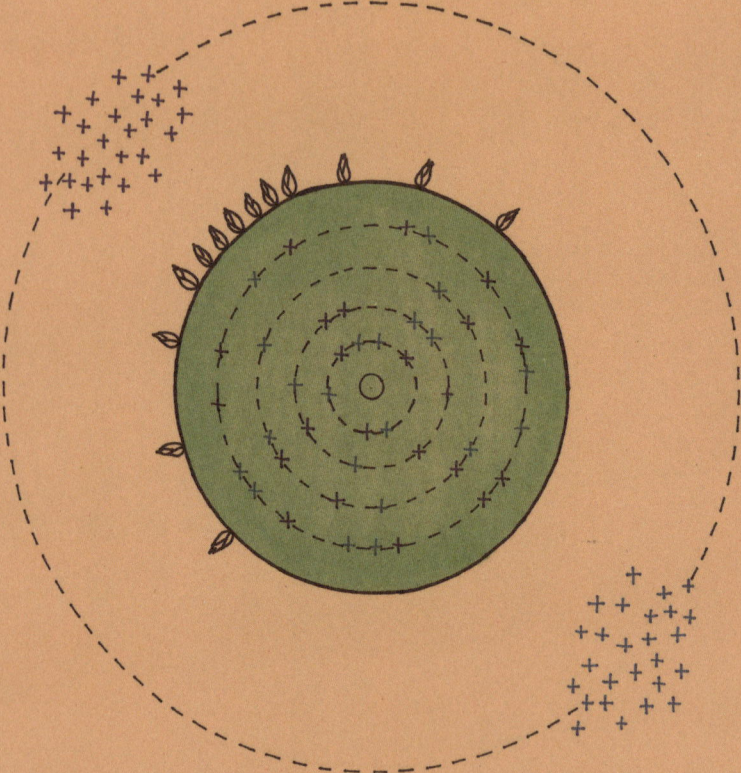

Rhythms of the Fields

Anastasia worked in an aubergine greenhouse in Westland
(the Netherlands) and followed the aubergine season to a
greenhouse in Almería (Spain).

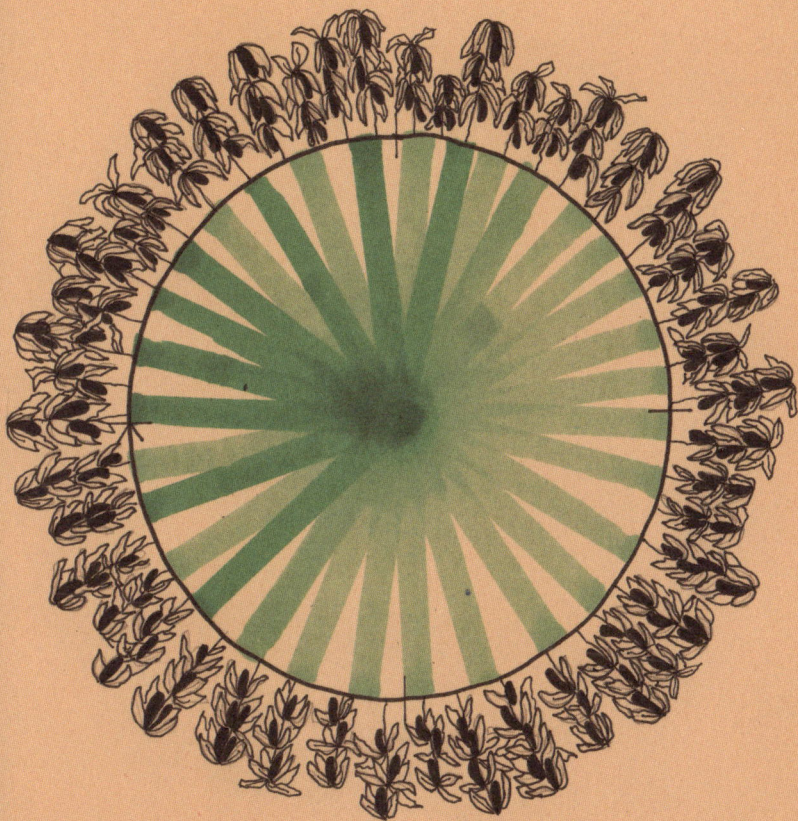

Prologue

Claire followed the movements of working bodies –
humans, insects and plants in a tomato greenhouse in
Veyrier (Switzerland).

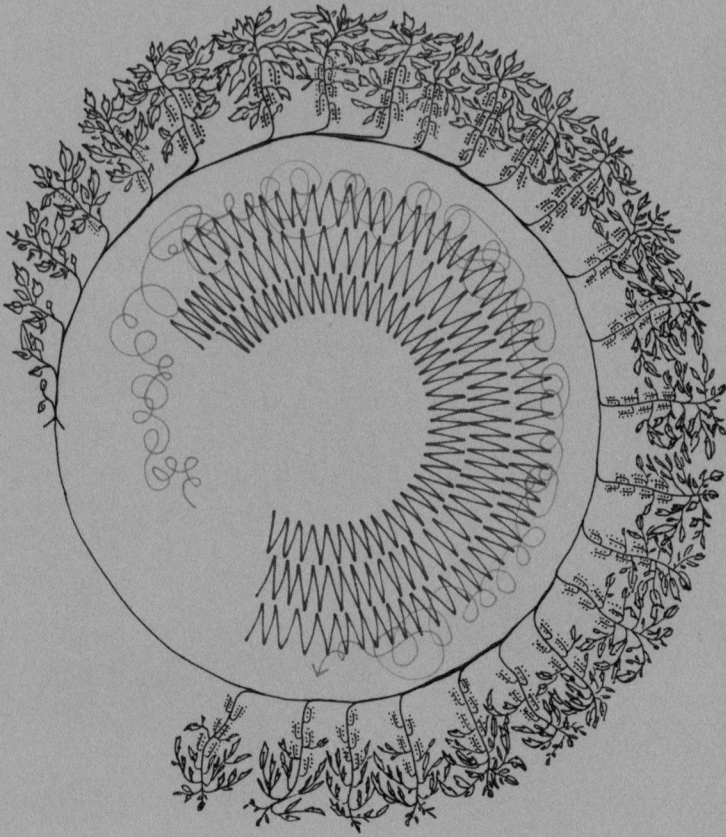

Rhythms of the Fields

Collectif dallas worked in a pear orchard in the north of France and learned about the tools and machines used to protect the crops from night frost in Haspengouw (Belgium).

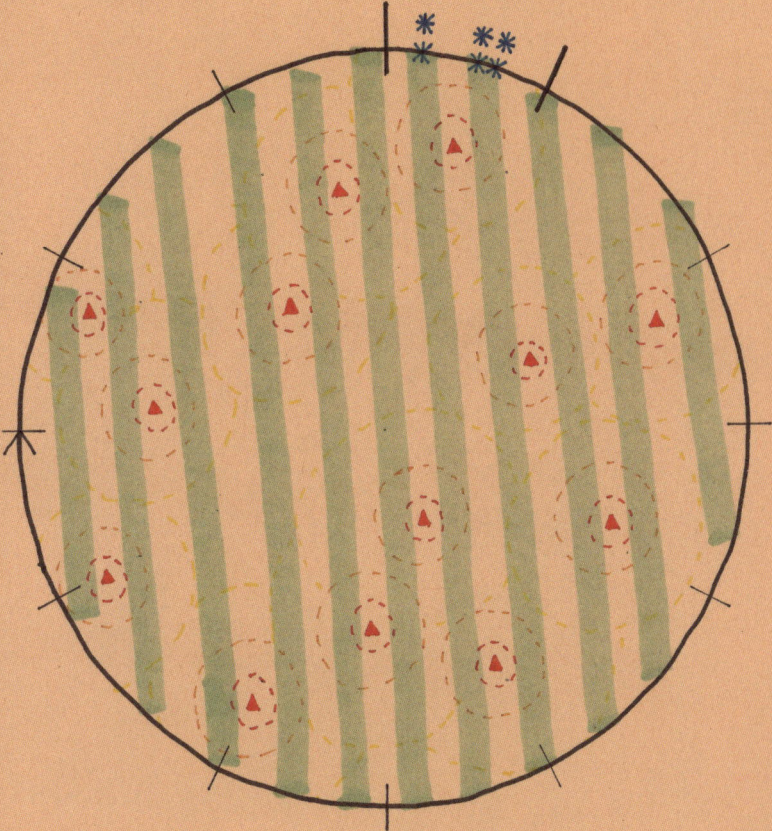

Ioana picked pumpkins and pears in the Netherlands and
revisited the village of her childhood summers in Romania.

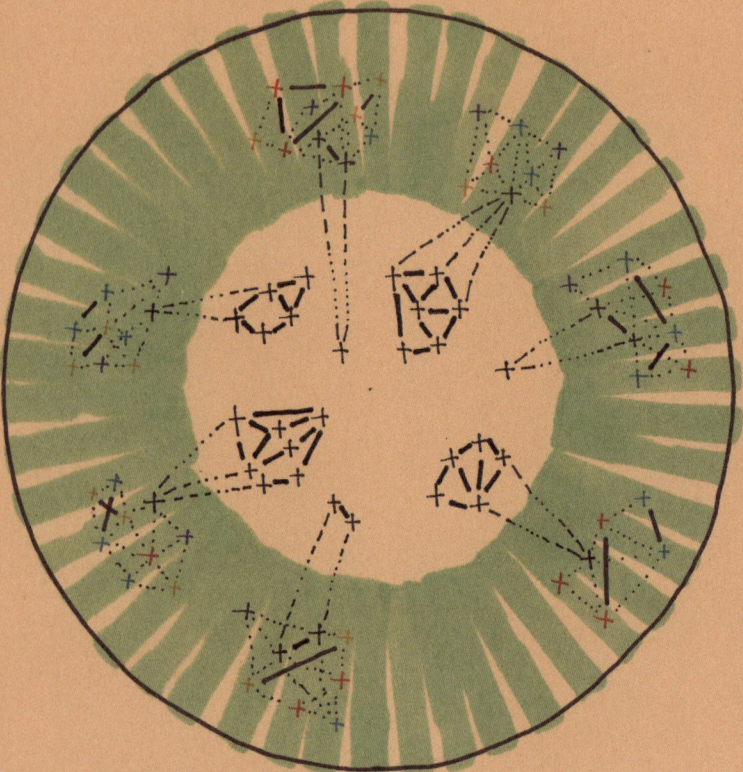

Rhythms of the Fields

Karolina worked on a vegetable farm in Poland alongside
Polish and Ukrainian workers and on a strawberry farm in
Flanders with seasonal workers from Poland.

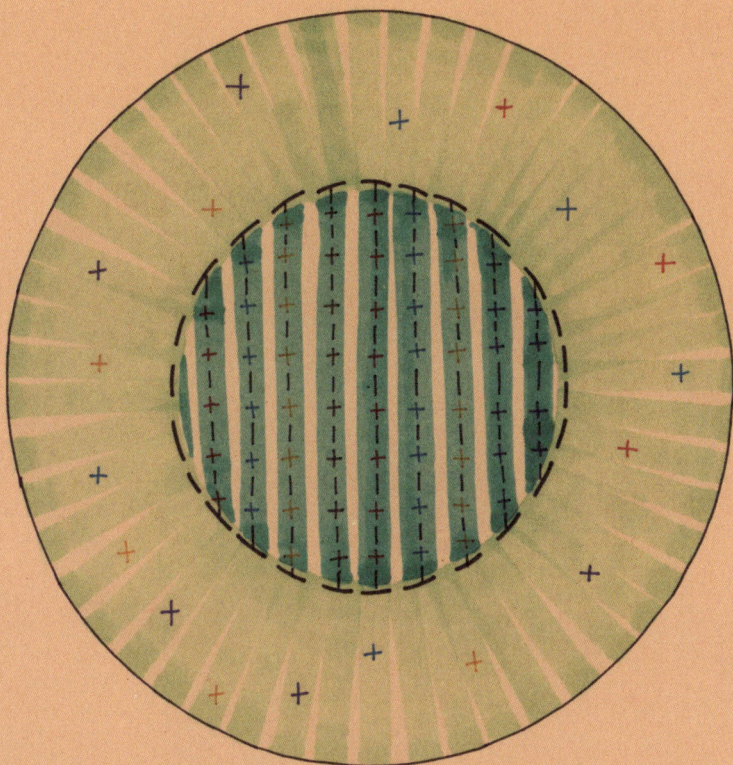

Prologue

Mona listened to the (mis)understandings of different languages in the fields of Haspengouw (Belgium).

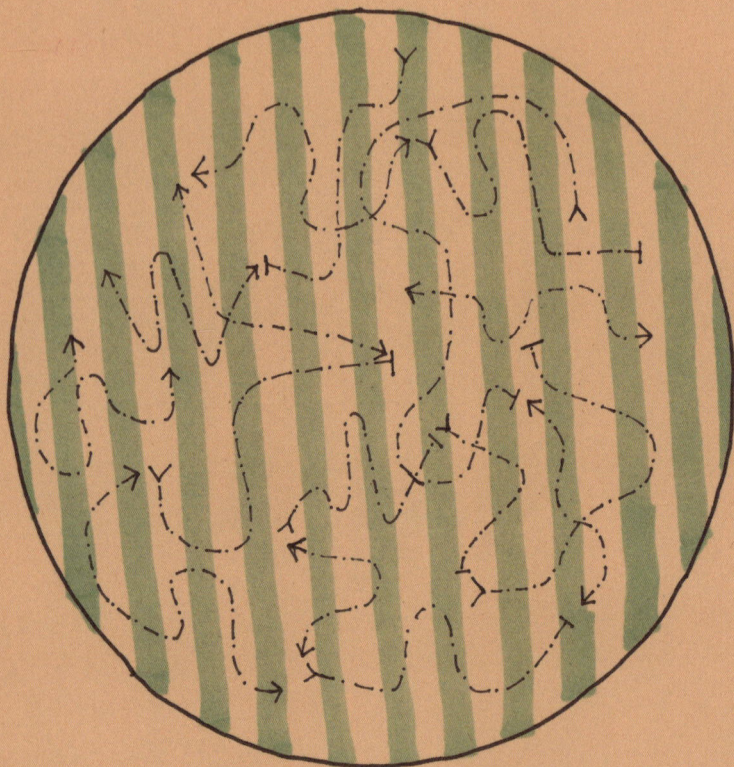

Yacinth worked in a pumpkin field in Ens (the Netherlands), paying attention to weeds growing among the productive plants.

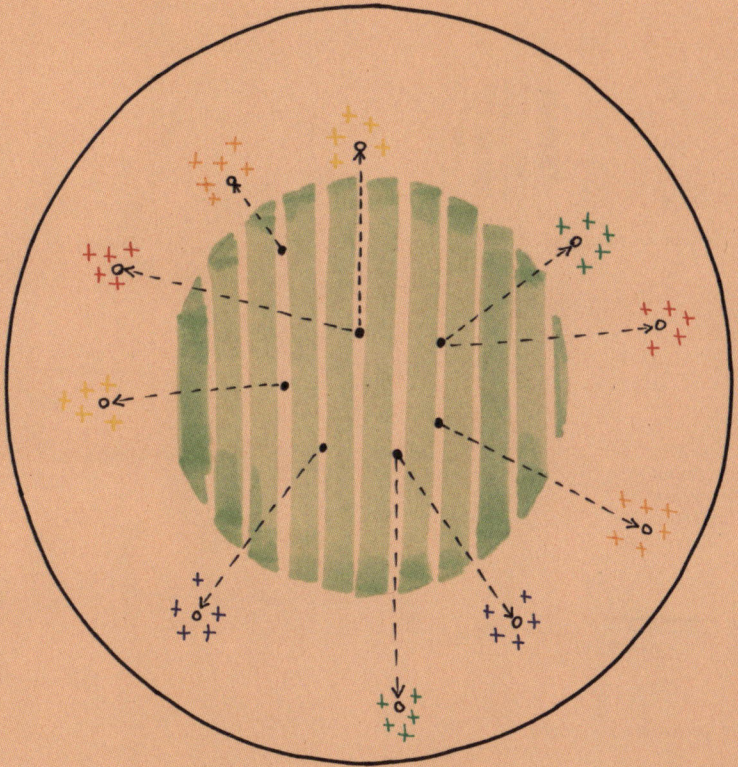

Prologue

Seasonal Neighbours' collaborative research originated from each member's work among seasonal workers in a field, orchard, greenhouse or other agricultural facility in the west of Europe. The maps attempt to record the steps between fieldwork and artwork, mapping a relationship that was crucial to the artists when starting their artistic process. In their multiplicity, the different maps gather the dynamics unfolding in these ruralities by tracing relationships, rhythms and exchanges between the many different human and more-than-human actors of the harvest.

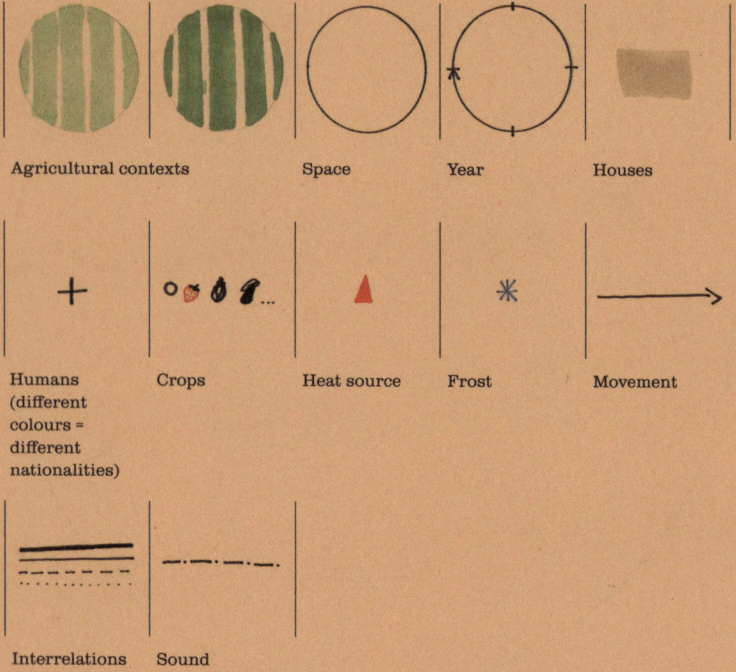

Agricultural contexts   Space   Year   Houses

Humans   Crops   Heat source   Frost   Movement
(different
colours =
different
nationalities)

Interrelations   Sound

Stories

TWO WEEKS IN LELYSTAD
BY IOANA

3 different farms
pumpkins, pears, weeds
slice with a knife, pull and pick with my hands,
    lay on a weeding bed to slice pumpkin stems
    and push pumpkin to the side
in total 70.5 work hrs at 10.78 euro/hr (after tax)

    it was supposed to be more than 80 when I
    applied... the weather made us lose 10 – 15 hrs
    that's 760 euros, take out 300 euros for food
    and accommodation, that's 460 euros for two
    weeks of hard work

*lost in translation... I ticked the wrong box on a
Dutch form and got taxed another 120 euros.
I was left with 340 euros... I hope to get the 120
euro back later in the year...

TO BE HERE

Three Fieldwork Short Stories

Jonathan De Maeyer,
Ciel Grommen and Ioana Lupascu

I
OH BOY

Place: a fruit farm with picker
accommodation in Kortenaken
Time: October 2022
Characters: Thomas, Bozena

It is dark but I am racing at high speed
through the steep roads of the Brabant
countryside. The roads are long and straight,
the villages far apart. The smell of damp
leafy greens, cut grass and cooled sun,
at the bottom of the hilly landscape, moves
quickly in and out of my nostrils. It's already ten o'clock in the evening. My bike is
overloaded and the deep potholes in the
invisible road make me sway violently. I am
scared as I haven't been in control of my
speed for a while. The trees at the top of the
hollow road block out the sky above my
head. I am crossing unfamiliar territory.
Kersbeek, Miskom, Vroente... Everyone
seems to be asleep already. Sweat dampens
my clothing.

      After a two-hour train ride and a
bike ride almost an hour long, I barely reach
the farm in Kortenaken, my destination.
I stumble around a courtyard. No one seems
to be awake. I have officially left my comfort
zone. The silence is uneasy in this unfamiliar
place. I tiptoe through a corridor and

finally find someone, a towering gray-haired
woman with bright clothes who breaks
the darkness of the narrow space we both
inhabit. Her name is Bozena and she speaks
a little Dutch. The intricate patterns of
her clothing draw my attention. With the de-
cisiveness of a caring mother she shows
me the bathroom, the kitchen and the bed-
rooms. I notice that this rough concrete
building is neither finished nor furnished.
My room has two unoccupied bunk beds.
Suddenly she says, 'Tomorrow we start at
half past seven', before leaving me to myself.

I know it's late but I had expected my
arrival to be different. I had imagined finding
everyone sitting cosily together in the
kitchen, like at the summer camps of my
youth. Instead, there is an unsettling silence.
I share the accommodation with twenty
other people I haven't seen yet. I'm nervous.
I hope tomorrow will bring more familiarity.

It's good to be back in my room. I wonder
about my *obichan* in Sweden. Will he have
to work on a farm as well? I hope he will
go to university like this boy. Will he realize
that I am doing this work to be able to see
him once a year?

Why does this boy cross the country
on his bike to come here and work with us?
Is there no work in the city? Are there no
other jobs in Belgium for students? My sew-

Stories

ing gear rests in the corner. I need to reinforce the knee pads once more. This evening
ritual makes me feel as if I'm still in control
of my inflamed joints.

I remember the first time I arrived
on this farm so I'll give this boy time to adapt.
Being surrounded by languages you don't
master is something you need to learn.
We've been working for a month and he has
yet to learn everything. I will have to take
him under my wing. I'm embarrassed by the
mess in the hallway, but he'll soon understand why it doesn't help to clean this place.
I hope he gets into the habit of taking off
his shoes at the entrance at least.

Around six o'clock, life gets going. Alarm
clocks in polyphonic ringtones pierce the
flimsy walls separating the rooms. There
is rumbling in the kitchen. I'm stuck in bed,
looking for my adventurous cheerfulness
from yesterday.

I slept badly. At night my thoughts go into
a never-ending loop of brooding over my
debts with Ioana, my plane ticket to Sweden,
someone ransacking my house... At half
past seven I'm outside and happy to start
work again. I'm ready for my favourite
moment of the day: putting on the picking
bags. It's not an easy thing to do. People
find I'm skilled at it and it's nice to be able

to help others. With my fingers, I smooth
the folds of the straps flat along their
shoulders. Small moments of attention and
care contrast with the toil of picking pears.

I don't dare to go downstairs yet. I have to!
This is why I'm here… I hear people in the
corridor. If they're downstairs I should go
too. Oh boy, why am I so shy? What's that
sound… Someone's flushing. Let's wait
another five minutes. I wonder how I ended
up in this situation. I don't feel at all prepared. How can you even prepare for something that is supposed to change you?
I want to surrender to the moment. Do I really
dare open myself up to unexpected twists
and turns? I try to remember similar moments in my life, but I can't find one. So I dig
down deeper in the sleeping bag and post-
pone the moment I have to get up. For the
first time, there is no safe distance between
where I am and what I am observing. Right
now, I am living in the middle of my subject.
I am part of my own research.

Where's the boy? I clearly said we were
starting work at seven thirty. Should I have
told him what time he should get up?
He's old enough. Why do I feel responsible
for him? A Bulgarian boy would never be
late on his first day.

The kitchen is practical. Large wooden tables fill the space, but there is no room for all the pickers at once. From the window, I can see the yard. A truck is loaded with boxes. When the gray jeep parks in the courtyard, everyone puts their shoes on.

> The weather doesn't look promising. The farmer decides that only the Bulgarians will go to the orchard. Sometimes I suspect him of favouring the Poles. But I won't complain, not today. In the orchard, I am at least sure I can work for ten hours. Since I'd like to leave before All Saints' Day this year, I need to work as many hours a day as possible. Let's see if I can make it.

As I walk from the residence to the hangar, I search for how to say 'good morning' in Polish but I keep forgetting. It's pouring rain so I'm assigned to the small sorting team back in the hangar. During work, there is almost no talk, nothing besides the weather. For now, 'rain' is the only Polish word I know. Luckily, smiling is the most important means of communication. We all do this together.

II
SILVER LININGS ON A
BED OF PUMPKINS

Place: a pumpkin field in Flevoland
Time: July 2021
Characters: Emi, Maria

I'm sitting in the back of a pickup truck
with six other workers. We're being driven
between harvest fields. There is an eerie
silence. Smiling, two other workers ride on
bikes behind the vehicle. It's a little too
crowded in the back, feet shuffling cutting
tools and dry mud from the day before.
We're heading to the pumpkin field.

> There is a new face among us, Emi, eagerly
> scanning the landscape. They're wearing
> pants that will just soak through at the first
> drop of rain and they'll get sick before the
> end of the week. The patch of Kabocha
> squash needs to be done by Friday and we're
> only seven. Do they even know how to do
> this job properly?

These Dutch farmlands used to be under
the sea not so long ago. Sand and soil were
used to fill the vastness of water in order
for crops to be able to grow. The flat landscape of Flevoland makes me miss home,

the hills, the messiness, the overbearing
hospitality. I've been in the Netherlands for
three years now taking on all sorts of jobs.
I'm familiar with this type of work and
its aches. I used to do it with the other kids
back home for our grandparents. We sold
the excess sour cherries from the garden to
a local business. We would compete with
each other and climb as high as possible in
the trees... to the distress of our mothers.
A box of cherries would bring in enough
money for a few ice-creams. I see the older
woman, Maria, studying me. Does she do
that with each new worker?

> There's something about them... Emi looks
> a bit too old to be a student. When they
> notice me watching, they smile at me with
> their mouths only. What kind of worker
> will they be? Do they even want to be here?
> Why are they fumbling around so much?
> I decide to ask. 'Are you a student?'

Maria passes me the tools. I'm struck by
her deep eyes. Our eyebrows look alike.
I follow the movement of her lips and realize
with a delay there was a question there.
I feel caught.

'Da ... un fel de ... Sorry, I mean, kind of ...
hmm.' I forget what language to use. I stut-
ter. There are many reasons, I think ...

I don't know. What answers is she looking for? Should I play the researcher? Or the student looking for extra work? Or should I tell her I was bored out of my mind in the cramped apartment? I desperately needed a distraction from my own thoughts. They get too dark too fast. In a frenzy I utter all I can to get the moment over with. My heart is racing, I feel like an impostor.

What is this vague answer? Are they trying to keep me off? We come from the same country, does Emi know that?! Why all this complexity and distrust? We're going to have to work together, so I ask again, but this leads to a stream of words that go way beyond my question. The others have already begun chopping away at the harvest. I try to keep up but they are speaking too fast. I see the farmer looking at us. Emi is still talking ... I move to the start of the harvest. 'Let me show you how it's done!'

I position myself with one foot on either side of the raised bed of soil. Gloves pulled on tightly, knife ready for action. 'Look ahead and visualize the end of the row', Maria says. She uses her right leg to draw an invisible arch from left to right and push away the leaves that expose the plum pumpkins. She then gently rolls the pumpkin to see the stem and cuts! I'm eager to prove my worth

as an East European labourer. Hard-
working, ready to take on any challenge,
to work through the pain, no complaining,
fast, fast, fast!

It's a sober act, not too much, not too little,
not too fast, not too slow. And treat the
pumpkins with the utmost caution. Is Emi
following? 'Pay attention. You've got to
keep up!'
      With this speed I'll end up having to
pick up the slack of the pickers this Satur-
day. I have my own plans. The clothes
market is only open in the morning on the
weekend. Plus, Mugur and Elena are coming by to see my new room. They're so excit-
ed, I guess I am too. I'm happy to finally
have a room of my own on this farm. 'Emi,
are you following?'

Maria looks like she's been around here
for a while. The other workers and even the
staff look at her with respect. She doesn't
smile easily but I can see she pays attention
to all the details.
     'Goedemorgen!', I hear in the back-
ground of my automatic movements. It's Jon,
the farmer. Please don't come my way,
I think to myself as the voice gets nearer,
please don't. He asks me my name and wants
to know if I'm OK. He's actually kind.
I decide to ask what to do with the blooming

dill flower. The smell is inebriating. 'Is it a weed or is it part of the crop?', I find myself saying too loudly. 'Maybe I can leave it here? It's dill, you know, tastes great in soups. And in dolmas!' 'Pull it out and leave it to the side', Jon answers with a smile as he slowly moves on to say hello to the other new pickers in the field. Is this his welcoming ritual? He heads to Maria, they seem to be having a tense conversation. She walks away, I follow her heavy steps as she checks if all the pumpkins have been cut away. I'm so cold and hungry already.

Jon is annoyed and accuses me of not having taken care of the rain jackets for the new recruits, but he should stop taking his frustrations with the agencies out on me. I know Jon chose the new agency because it seems to manage this whole business better... but he's rather naive in that regard. The workers' situation won't change much until the bigger system changes.

I'm not in the mood for any attitude so I sternly shift the conversation back to what is my responsibility. His eyes are pinning me for speaking back. I won't give in, not anymore. It's been six years... Should I care that he is trying to be a better farmer? I don't owe him that, even if he is nice.

The wetness is wrinkling my toes, but there's nothing I can do about it. Raindrops cloud my glasses and I realize I must have been stuck like this for more than a minute. I catch myself watching Maria's actions, movements and posture. I want her to like me. 1 try to copy her crafted way of placing the pumpkin in the cart. After an hour I hear a whistle and Maria's voice resonates across the field. My lower back muscles clench to my spine. I squat to ease the pain.

'Let's go! The rain is too heavy! We'll have lunch early today.' I can see people dragging their feet to the pickup car, dragging out time... when you work for months on end, the work becomes mundane, boring and too hard. I know all too well the strategy of stretching time to get paid a bit more. Judging by the clouds, we probably won't be able to keep working today. I don't even know what I can say to them this time... There are no minimum hours to be paid. If the weather's bad, you send the workers home.

Mugur and Elena keep telling me that I'm better off working directly with the farmers, no agency involved, proper pay. I want to tell them it's lonely sometimes, being the only foreigner. I don't dare, since I know working with an agency during the rainy weeks barely covers the rent of the pickers' accommodation. 'Let's go!'

We jump in the pickup and hurry back to the warehouse. By now it's pouring. My dirty boots make puddles around them. I place my tool bag on top. Viorica, one of the other Romanian workers, sees it and gives me a sneaky grin. She says she and Maria are cousins. Viorica and I were assigned to the weeding bed the other week. We found ourselves laughing and rolling our eyes when one of the other workers started talking about 'the good old days' in Eastern Europe, when communism was in full bloom and factories provided work in one's own country. It felt nice to speak a language that belonged to just us in a place that feels so far. Her kids are my age, also working in the Netherlands. 'Good kids', she proudly said. I want to ask her what Maria's story is. I don't dare yet.

We shelter while we wait for the rain to stop. Maria fills in the slips for the day, I can see she added an extra half hour to our rota. Did she also start as a picker? I roll a cigarette to end the work day. Maria and Viorica join me for a smoke. There isn't much to say but I feel at ease.

III
TOO SOFT A SKIN

Place: a pear orchard in Borgloon
Time: August 2017
Characters: Lotte, Alicja

In the orchard, the pear trees are planted so tight that their branches create a dense canopy that blocks the horizon. Every thirty metres, we come across a wooden crate called a 'palox', which we fill by carefully releasing the elastic band of our picking bags and sliding the apples inside. It's a task repeated rhythmically. I used to observe these orchards from the field court of my childhood school, pedalling slowly by their vastness. But now, after many years, I find myself in the midst of this corridor of pear trees, taking on a job as a picker, school years far behind me.

I've been assigned to a new team: Samet, Camil and Esra. The women pick the lower branches of the tree with a step. The men follow with their ladders to do the tops. I marvel at how many kilos those thin twigs can bear! Dewdrops slide from my hand down my arm into the sleeves of my Mackintosh coat. Sometimes I try to pull off two pears at once, but it doesn't actually make it any faster.

Things work well here, I find, but my team
members sigh frequently. I seek eye contact,
hoping for a smile, but all I get is an ac-
knowledging nod. Only slowly did I realize
that we all have a different mother tongue.
I speak Dutch, Samet is Bulgarian of Turkish
heritage, Camil speaks Polish, and Esra
Romanian. 'Polish mafia?', I wink, pointing
at Camil's fancy sunglasses. It turns out
to be a joke everyone understands. The ice
has been broken.

> Why am I so unlucky? I'm surrounded by
> people that have forgotten how to have fun.
> Yolo! They don't get it. I'm happy that yes-
> terday evening people stayed in the kitchen
> to eat the birthday cake I made, but why
> was there such a fuss about going dancing
> together afterwards? Only Uma and Camil
> wanted to join me. Drinking shots with the
> locals, we made the most of it until mid-
> night. On the way back, I saw Mandek trying
> not to laugh at our jokes. I wish he wasn't
> the only one with a car. He's so protective of
> it. He won't say so, but I'm sure he was
> happy he had to drive.

I hear laughter from a colleague in the lane
alongside us. From his ladder, he has seen a
branch land in the face of Samet, who is
now cleaning the green from his face. Oops,
I must have pulled a little too hard! It

inspires Esra, who's standing below Camil's ladder, to fiercely shake the branches and throw him off balance. Our laughter attracts the attention of the foreman. Alicja and Mandek appear at the end of the queue with curious looks. Mandek carries his picking bag nonchalantly by his side. Polish pop music echoes from his phone. We nod and continue harvesting dutifully. Alicja casually walks past us. She winks at me then checks the pears in the palox for blisters.

After an hour, the first paloxes have been filled. Everyone seems to have started well. Leon gets his tractor to drive the harvest to the trailer. I hoped the quietness of the morning would last a bit longer. As I take a tasty bite of a pear, I hear Yvette shouting in the distance. I run to her and see her arranging a ladder demonstratively against a tree. Asparoech stands next to the farmer's wife, staring silently at the ground. 'What's wrong?' The old man mutters that he's afraid of heights. I translate and Yvette exclaims incredulously, 'Well, that's a first!', one of her favourite sayings. I suggest that Asparoech could swap with Agatha, who's already a long way down the row picking the bottom pears. Yvette is so stuck in her habits sometimes. Why wouldn't a woman be able to work with a ladder anyway?

It's getting warmer and warmer. My smart-
phone reads 27 degrees, with not a cloud in
sight. Sweat pours from my face, arms and
belly staining all that I wear. My water bottle
is packed in my backpack at the beginning
of the row, far behind us, just like the half-
hour lunch break. The usual ten-minute
break around three o'clock is not coming.
I'm terribly thirsty. Aren't the others?

Today we have to pick Doyenné pears, very
tasty but soft and vulnerable. We don't have
these pears at home. If a single one ends
up in the palox with a rotten spot, they'll all
be for waste. We have a hard time supervis-
ing. Yvette and Mandek seem to be losing
patience and their instructions have turned
to shouting. I get the Belgian girl in my
sight. She's quietly languishing, disappearing into herself, as so often happens when
someone doesn't have the physical strength
for this kind of work. Her face is red and
pale at the same time. It must be new to her.
'Are you tired?' I ask her.

How should I reply? Normally I'm a hard
worker who rarely gets tired, but today I have
to give in.
'Yes, I'm tired' I sigh, but immediately
I realize how silly this sounds, compared to
the rest of the team that's been here for

weeks. 'But it's OK!' I add. 'Are you tired?'
Alicja looks straight into my eyes.

'I? Uh ...' I think about the dancing last
night and how much good it did me. I laugh
and answer: 'Yes, I'm tired, but tiredness
is my friend!'

Alicja walks on with a confident gait.
Her blonde ponytail springs up and down.
Her drive motivates me. I learned from
the others that her mother tongue is Polish,
but she speaks Russian with the Bulgarians
and English with the farmers and me.
I'm the only Belgian picker.

She hooks me with her eyes as I turn ...
It strikes me that she still managed to ask
something in return. Kindness and hospitality between overcoming fatigue? She's
a local, this blonde girl with blue trainers,
I can tell. She's a good one. Kind. It makes
me realize why I treasure this work here,
away from the abstractions and complexities
of my office job in Poland. Juggling with
the psychology of administrators and
bureaucratic loopholes. Here, at least, everyone holds the same dirt in their hands.

'Pauze!', Alicja calls.
Finally! My watch reads 3:20 p.m.
We keep our picking bags on and walk fast

toward our backpacks. Mandek, the older foreman, calls out something. Everyone returns in silence with shoulders drooping. Is this *pauze* abolished!? I really needed that water! Who actually makes the rules here?

> Yes, I'm tired! Tired of having my call undermined by Mandek. Why can't the people have a break? If we're going to have to continue late anyways, we need these ten minutes to cheer everyone up. It's his pride again. He constantly wants to show off how he has made a career here in Belgium. We know his talk about the younger generation and their lack of work mentality. Luckily, we know better. We no longer want to be the low-wage workers of Europe. The Bulgarians, on the other hand, always obey. They probably have no other choice and Mandek enjoys that!

I suddenly notice that some of the youngsters have sat down angrily and shout back indignantly. I learn that *'Dostatochno!'* means 'Enough!', but I don't know in what language. I hesitate for a second, sympathize with the activists, then walk back to my group to continue harvesting the pears, feeling like I have no choice but to obey. When I climb up Samet's ladder and my head towers above the orchard, I dwell on my

own docility. Why didn't I join them?
I actually admire them for revolting.

The plan in my head looked good: join
the harvest and get to know my seasonal
neighbours. I thought we could exchange
feelings of uprootedness and I would ask
their opinion about artistic representations
of those feelings, but I didn't count on the
work being so overpowering. I didn't consider
losing every ability to think. If this work
robs me of my thinking powers, why am I
actually still doing it? The work is still paid
by the hour. The contracts are renewed
on a daily basis. I could stop and walk home
right now.

My gaze meets Samet's, who has
just emptied his picking bag at the palox.
I learned from his Facebook page that
he alternates this work with pruning in the
vineyards of France and sorting work in
a Dutch greenhouse. What would it be like
to do this work for several months, let
alone year-long?

I stand next to Fatima and Jamil. Everyone
knows Fatima is fighting her rheumatism to
pay for her husband's surgery. Jamil had to
sell all his cows. He desperately needs this
job to simply pay for his food. The mentality
of pushing through the day makes me question who benefits ultimately.

'Don't you realize that some of the people around could be your parents?', I ask Mandek, the son of the first generation of seasonal workers in Belgium.

Mandek looks at me. Pop music continues echoing from his phone. He knows he's gone too far. He turns to the group and concedes. 'OK, you can have a drink, but we're not taking another break today.'

Three fictional short stories delve into the realm of seasonal agricultural labour in Belgium (Flanders) and the Netherlands. The stories start out from the fieldwork experiences of Jonathan De Maeyer, Ciel Grommen and Ioana Lupascu. By examining the shared threads woven through their encounters, the stories reveal striking similarities in their presence on the job, hinting at their conditioning, artistic inclinations and intellectual engagement.

The collective aim of this writing experiment is to portray the intricate relationships and connections that emerge between individuals within the context of a picking field. It touches on themes of isolation, care, friendship, intimacy and curiosity, while also looking into the broader implications of power dynamics and the often overlooked aspects of agricultural settings.

To Be Here

CHANGING LANDSCAPES

Stills from an Unfinished Film

Jonathan De Maeyer
and Maximiliaan Royakkers

...Time goes by...

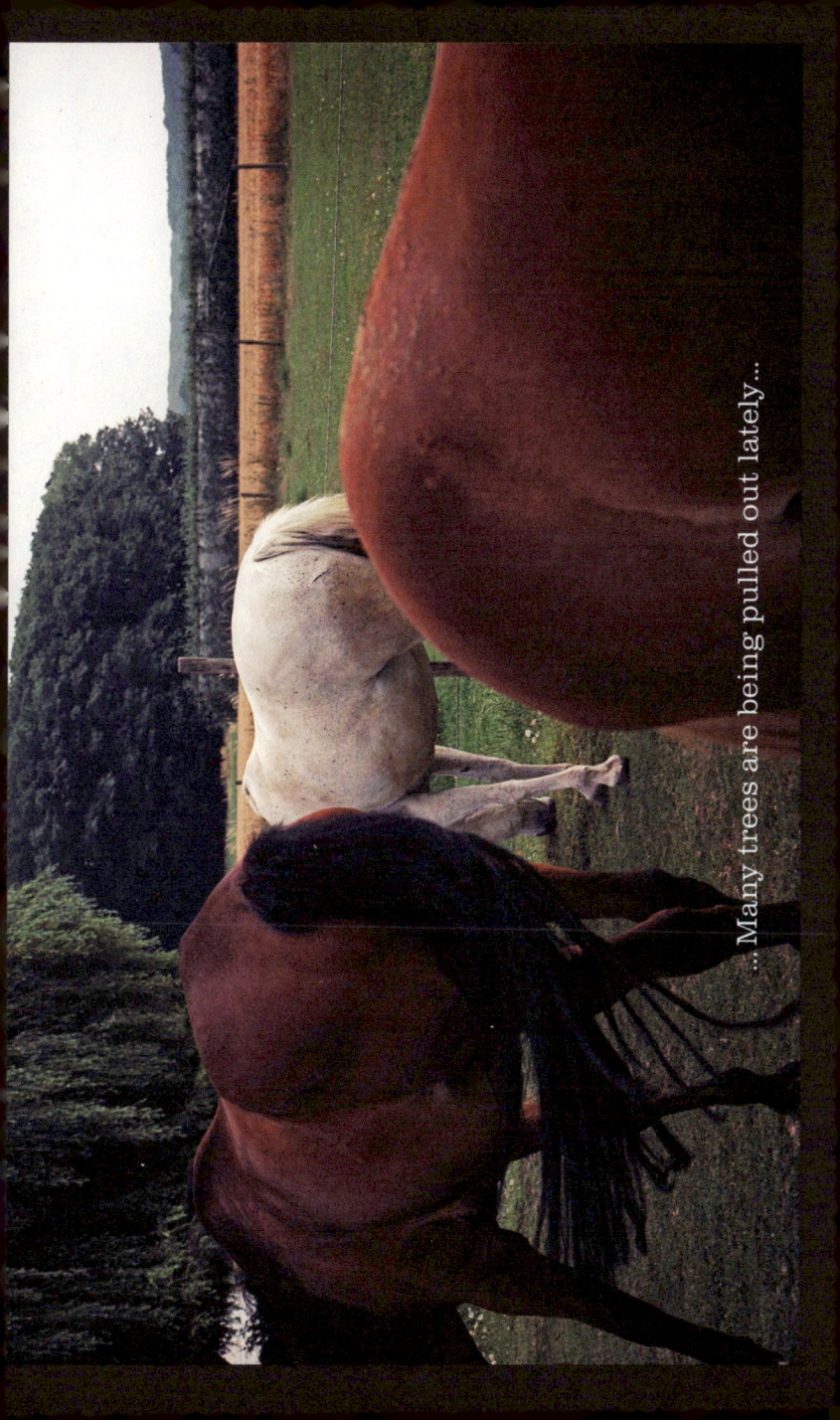

...Many trees are being pulled out lately...

...It appears they will place the wind turbines in the valley...

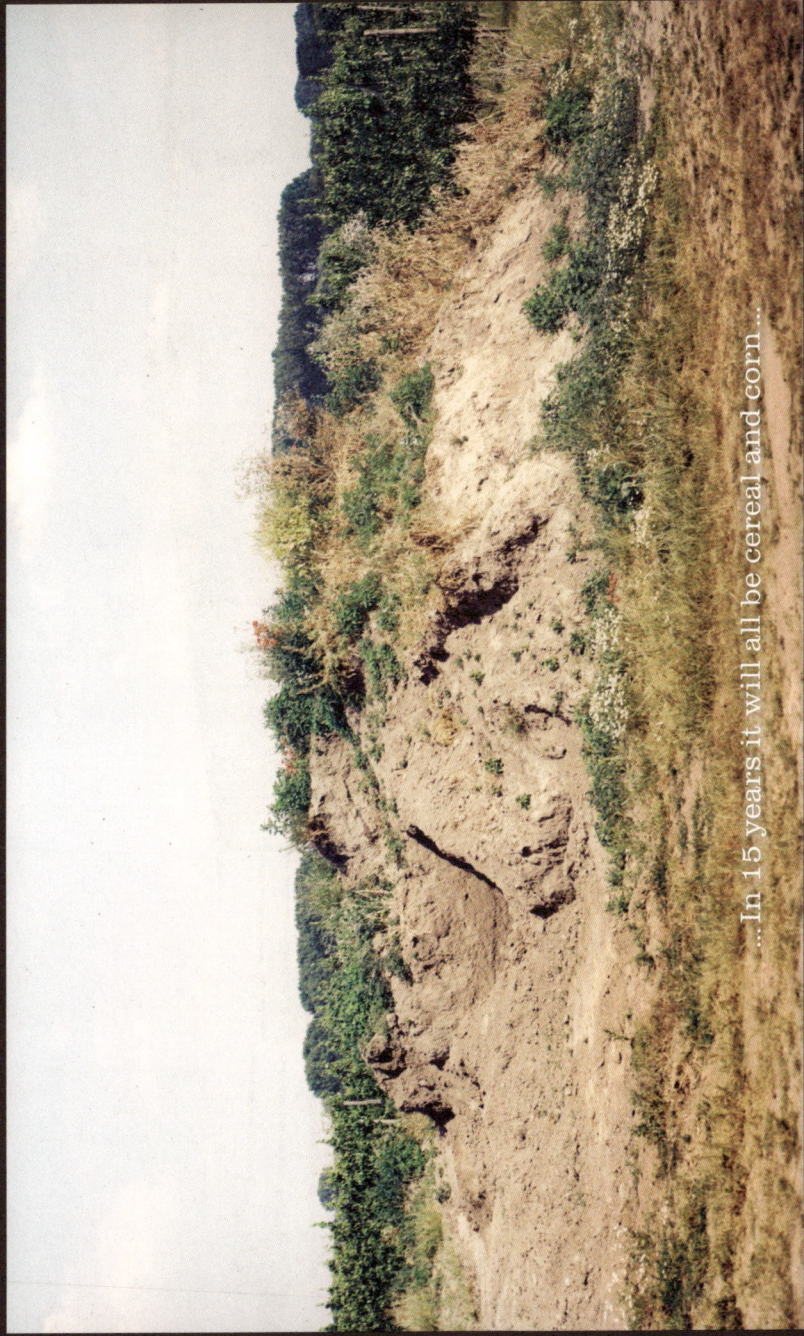

...In 15 years it will all be cereal and corn...

...All kinds of fruit are brought here to be packed and shipped...

...Mainly to the Far East and South East Asia ...

...Small ends, bigger gets bigger...

...It's still quiet now...

...But on summer mornings I hold out my hand and then they stick their thumbs up in the air ...

...Sometimes I see them through the rows of trees, sometimes I see them sitting on their tractors ...

...My hands are not made to pick...

... I don't like Jonagold ...

Using a 24 km hiking loop as their guideline, Maximiliaan Royakkers and Jonathan De Maeyer revisit the rural town of Kortenaken and the area around the apple and pear orchards where Jonathan conducted fieldwork in 2021. As rural *flâneurs*, they capture the landscape in a subdued photographic style and collect descriptions of the area through casual conversations with local residents, the direct neighbours of the orchards and farms. Brimming with commonplace opinions and personal anecdotes, these short testimonies inspired the artists to compose a series of visual short stories, each consisting of one still image. The result is a conspicuous unwinding of the predispositions as to how we perceive rural landscapes around us.

Changing Landscapes

AGRICULTURE IS NOT AN INDUSTRY

Conversation with Arnd Spahn

Anastasia Eggers and Ciel Grommen

Arnd Spahn is an experienced German trade union-ist who works in the sector of European Agricul-ture. He served for twenty-two years as Agricultural Political Secretary for EFFAT, the European Fed-eration of Food, Agriculture and Tourism Trade Unions. Ciel Grommen and Anastasia Eggers sat down with him to discuss the many challenges con-cerning the social and legal position of seasonal workers in relation to national and international regulations, or the lack thereof.

SN: Could you start by explaining
what EFFAT is and does precisely?

AS: EFFAT is the European Federation of Food, Ag-riculture and Tourism Trade Unions. This concerns the whole food chain, from the field to the table, including the processing of food, restaurants, pub-lic gastronomy, catering and so on. Under tourism we understand restaurants and hotels, but it also includes mountain guides and ski teachers.

EFFAT represents 116 national trade unions from 37 European countries, so our scope is not only the European Union (EU) but the European conti-nent. We inform the member unions about priori-ties and developments in Europe and defend the interests of more than twenty-five million workers before the European institutions, European em-ployer associations and transnational companies.

> Can you describe in general terms the
> role of seasonal workers in agriculture
> in Europe?

To start with, 'seasonal workers' is a rather vague term. There are a lot of national definitions, but there is no European understanding. The Seasonal Workers Directive (2014/36/EU) gives a definition, but this directive is only linked to certain third-country nationals, not to intra-EU migrants. We therefore prefer the term 'mobile workers'. In Italy, for example, we see a lot of internal mobility, or what we call 'time-limited' work, and refers to workers travelling within the country from south to north following the different crops (olives, fruit and vegetables, citrus fruit, wine, etc.). This type of work is often performed by illegal workers, refugees and East European workers. These travelling workers don't label themselves as 'seasonal' workers. Applying the term 'mobile workers' makes it possible to include them in the work done by EFFAT.

> Can you compare the challenges of
> agricultural seasonal work to seasonal
> work in other domains?

Tourism is another sector in which the seasonality of labour occurs, yet the highest rate of seasonal work is definitely in agriculture. The geographical area that EFFAT focuses on covers ten million dependent workers, four million of who are cross-border migrant workers. With 40 %, agriculture is the sector with the highest international mobility rate of all sectors in Europe. The nature of agricultural seasonal work is highly specific. The main goal of most seasonal workers is to make a lot of money in a very short time. This way the workers can return home and feed their family, and maybe in the long run build a house or start a business in their own country. Often, seasonal work is a better economic alternative than the options in their place of origin. In other sectors and industries, worker ambitions are very different.

It is important to stress that seasonality is not a man-made concept, but that it is determined by the earth and the sun, so we shouldn't simply adjust the definition based on employers' needs. For example, Christmas is not a season, but a holiday, of literally one day, agreed by society. A robust discussion is taking place in Europe today as regards broadening the definition of seasonality in the interest of companies like Amazon and other delivery services. This would allow them to open up their labour relations to legal seasonal definitions, speaking about the 'Christmas season', for instance. EFFAT firmly opposes this as it would only mean that more people would be plunged into the precarious situation of seasonal work we are precisely trying to fight. In addition, the social problems associated with seasonal work are intrinsically linked to specific historical developments in agriculture, so we should avoid expanding it to other sectors. For example, a century ago, 80 % of the Belgian population worked in agriculture, two centuries ago it was 95 %. Traditionally, seasonal workers came from the region itself.

> It is interesting that you talk about
> the origins of seasonal migrant work
> two centuries ago, while the collective
> research of Seasonal Neighbours
> was tracing it back to the moment the
> European labour markets opened.
> Are there important historical events
> that were decisive for the development
> of seasonal work?

Seasonal migration started in 1750 but really only developed after 1850 with the Industrial and French Revolutions. At that time there was a big rural exodus, as growing cities offered more opportunities, freedom and individual possibilities. As a result, the availability of local hands to work in agriculture was severely reduced. In East Germany we can still find historical buildings, the so-called *Schnitterkasernen* or 'reaper barracks', built to house Polish seasonal workers since the 1780s. Similar infrastructures can be found in Spain.

The establishment of the EU changed a lot of course, but wars in particular were a cause of increased migration. For example, after World War I there were ten times more seasonal workers in Germany than before, with people coming from Poland, what was then Belarus, Ukraine, etc. After World War II, hundreds of thousands of people migrated northwards, for example, from Spain to France. When I was young, I had my first job as fruit picker in a French winery. I remember that at the time, there was a very strict hierarchy inside the different groups of seasonal workers. From the moment there weren't enough people from the south, the market was opened to Latin America in Spain, France, Belgium and Portugal.

The end of colonialism, around 1965, also had a big impact on agriculture. Millions of people from the former colonies migrated to the 'mother' countries, where they faced exclusion from local and regional labour markets. So they had to take whatever work was available, and seasonal work was often one of the few possibilities.

Another decisive moment was the fall of the Berlin Wall, when East European citizens could travel more easily, not as refugees but as tourists. A striking example are the figures in Spain from 1995 to 2007: roughly 3.5 million people migrated from Romania to Spain, of who 1.5 went to work in agriculture. At the end of this period, in 2007, there were 800,000 registered Romanians working in Spanish agriculture, while one year later, the year Romania entered the EU, there were none left – on paper. Of course, nothing changed in reality – Spanish agriculture still depends for 95 % of people from abroad – but the 'miracle' of Spanish statistics changed the way it is presented. Spain no longer wanted to be informed about this group of people. If there are no official figures, these people simply cannot appear in political statements. The absurdity is that the only agricultural migrant workers the Spanish statistics are 'collecting' are the illegal ones.

> When speaking about the 'illegal ones', do you mean the African workers that are heavily involved in Spanish and Italian agriculture? How is their situation different from, for example, European workers?

The illegal workers are the unregistered migrants and refugees. These do not coincide on a one-to-one basis with all workers coming from African countries. Some are fully registered as the result of the bilateral agreements which EFFAT has been involved in since the 1980s. We have a strong structure developed for Moroccans to enter the European agricultural labour market: a clear budget, limited numbers, but some of the workers have well-organized counter-systems. The refugee market is also very well organized. Every structure creates its own system.

According to the head of the department of the Italian Ministry of Agriculture, a farmer who wants to respect Italy's social regulations has no access to seasonal workers. This means that in this country, the structure has created its own system of illegality. In 2020, however, the anti-*caporalato* or 'anti-gangmaster' law was introduced in Italy resulting in more than one hundred *caporalato* being put in prison, meaning the country is on its way to developing more socially acceptable structures.

Another example is Portugal, which opens doors to Latin America, because of their colonial history there. Based on bilateral agreements, they are legally allowed to open their national labour market, but in reality they often send these people to other European countries, like France. This means that they have started to act as gangmasters, earning money from human trafficking. For ten years EFFAT has worked on this case, stating that a bilateral law cannot lead to the opening of the European labour market, since it is an agreement between a sending country and a host country only. These examples show that every region is different, so EFFAT's answers and actions are always tailor-made.

> What is your political vision regarding the organization of seasonal work in agriculture?

I'm very neutral on the question of the existence of seasonal migrant work. I'm neither for nor against. Neither am I against working with refugees or illegals ... Every country has its own history and has to look for different solutions.

There are of course phenomena in agriculture such as slavery and forced labour as well as structural child labour, that are unacceptable. But they cannot be addressed by making a law that would stop such labour. Because we are not speaking about what we call an 'industry'. We are speaking of very long traditions and historical self-understanding of people involved in agriculture that are woven into those structures. In Europe we have more farms than all enterprises across all economic sectors in all member states combined! We have more than 14 million farms in Europe. Compare this to food processing, which has only 220,000 enterprises. And yet these 220,000 enterprises generate more money than 14 million farms.

'Circular migration' is a great concept that refers to how seasonal work has been organized ever since. When a farmer needs helping hands, he first looks for people in his own family or the local area. When the people living in rural areas have better alternatives, the farmers have to look in the wider region, on a national level, and finally on an international level. So according to this concept, the geographical circles around the farm gradually enlarge.

Today however, this circular movement is increasingly being lost by organizing work via intermediaries (gangmasters or interim companies, the 'legal' gangmasters). This means hiring people from anywhere. The consequence is that their integration is no longer considered and this, in my experience, always leads to more inhumane conditions. For example, countries are slowly opening up their labour markets to Chinese workers through agreements with the Chinese government. They bring people from China directly to the farms accompanied by organized 'security' rather similar to a police force: the guards are armed and prevent people from leaving the premises. This kind of structure makes employers think that there won't be any problems with people falling sick or wanting to stay or whatnot, or at least that it will no longer be the employer's problem. Therefore, EFFAT has started a campaign against these 'Chinese police forces'.

Moreover, today seasonal workers are too much considered as a group, and only for the duration of their contract, after what they have to return, denying any future possibility of integrating them. It is evident that these workers then tend to say 'I can do whatever I want, nobody cares'. But being an employer myself, I am convinced that it is crucial to recognize the capacity of the individuals you are working with. Many migrant workers are more resilient when it comes to doing agricultural work than local workers, who often look for opportunities elsewhere, and therefore they are able to help solve the many problems rural societies face. Also, government structures must support the development of individual capacities for the particular problems rural areas are experiencing nowadays, through what we call lifelong learning programmes and such.

In the EU, there is free movement of labour, so there is a clear ambition to organize labour on a European scale. On the other hand, labour policy is still a national affair. What is the logic behind this? Should Europe play a bigger role?

Europe is playing an increasingly strong role. Labour policy is no longer organized only on a national level. There are a lot of European strategies and directives, for example on health and safety in the workplace. European regulation serves as a frame for every member state. It is not yet enough, but you have to understand that mobility within the European labour market is nowhere as strongly developed as in agriculture. To illustrate: the sectors with the highest international mobility rate are agriculture, transport and construction, but if we compare these figures, it is 40 % in agriculture, and about 7 % in construction. The main reason for this difference is the phenomenon of 'corridor migration' encountered in agriculture, meaning Belgian agriculture hires Polish workers, Polish agriculture hires Belarusian or Ukrainian workers and so on. This is not yet the case in other sectors.

Are there any specific trends in seasonal work that can be linked directly to industrialisation and upscaling in agriculture?

Yes, of course it changes a lot for agricultural work. For one thing, increased mechanization has led to a reduction of horrible work conditions. Machines and tools are increasingly performing work that is unacceptable for humans. For instance, in Germany the *Gurkenflieger* or 'cucumber plane', a machine in which people lie 30 cm above the ground in order to pick cucumbers, is going to be replaced by robot arms.

On the other hand, large-scale agriculture has a devastating effect on social relations in rural areas. The industrial production of tomatoes in South Italy is one of the most unacceptable situations we have in Europe at present. The people who are working here are 100 % illegal, 100 % refugees. They work for 50 cents per hour and live in unacceptable conditions, today, in Europe! But it's not so easy to solve this economically. To put it simply, the price of industrial tomatoes is now 40 cents per kilo. In China, our direct competitor, the production costs are between 6 and 8 cents per kilo.

We tried to work on solutions but what do you do: blame the employers, blame the consumers? That just doesn't work. What we really need is to have a thorough political discussion on how to solve a socially unacceptable situation. The other option is to stop this type of production and import everything from China, but then again this implies that we accept their standards.

So yes, raising the efficiency of agricultural production with more mechanization and automation looks like a good option for the economy and for reducing inhumane labour conditions, which might also not be so good for the environment. But this is speaking from my own perspective as a trade unionist, defending the situation of the workers. I'm not an expert in environmental impact. I'm the first to say that environmental impact should be regulated and integrated in upcoming policies, like all the other aspects of sustainable development: social policies, sustainable economies and so on. It shouldn't be either/or.

Are the migrant workers represented by the national labour unions? Based on our experience, seasonal migrant workers are seen as competitors rather than as fellow workers by domestic workers.

Yes, sometimes more so, sometimes less. There is not one country where there is enough representation. As a federation, our policy is to say to our labour unions that they are responsible for the workers who are working in the area where they have legal responsibility, regardless of their background, religion, gender or other. Sometimes, when labour unions fail to take this responsibility, migrant workers manage to organize themselves in national migrant worker initiatives. This is interesting because it allows us to establish official relations to these structures. Otherwise, if not, we have to go out and try to figure out where they are. This is no easy task. We usually start with church-based initiatives: orthodox priests from Eastern Europe in Spain or the Netherlands, Sikh temples in Southern Italy, etc. When there is a possibility to build structures, we support the organization of smaller communities. We can then send our agents and experts there once in a while to give advice and inform them about social security, pensions, how to send money to their families, etc. If they are not self-organized, the situation is always more difficult.

In order to reach the workers more effectively, EFFAT has been working on an app that was launched in April 2023, *season@work*. It exists in eleven languages (Bulgarian, Arabic, Portuguese, Spanish, etc.). You can choose the country you want to work in and find a lot of videos and additional information on contracts and so on. I'm sure this is the future of communication for seasonal workers, because all the other instruments are too text-based and fail to reach the workers effectively.

Lastly, as a collective we're mainly interested in the relations between farmers, seasonal workers and local communities. Do you think local communities can play a role? Have you seen any opportunities for change in that respect?

In the past, local communities had a strong interest in seasonal workers. Today this interest is lower than ever in history, because the communities are not seeing enough good examples of how to integrate them. It's the same with refugees: they're seen as part of a problem, not part of a solution. If communities are engaged, it is because they saw a bad example in the press, but rarely because they see chances and opportunities in integrating them.

Seasonal workers are familiar with working and living in rural areas, this means they have their own skills and knowledge. But they can only contribute locally if you give them the chance to self-organize and become integrated! At the least, you have to protect them from any official discrimination. By giving them opportunities, some open space, a little support and such, they can develop their own structures within a given community and integrate more rather than remain invisible and alien to the places they are working in.

SOMETIMES I DREAM OF CHICORY

Soms Droom ik van Witloof

Pia Jacques

sit likes a tongue
in the serpent's mouth

All creations
and destruction
are but momentary
shaddow of
phenomena.

In mindfulness beginnen met ademen
Toegangkelijke beginstappen
voor gewone mensen

door Buddhadāsa Bhikkhu

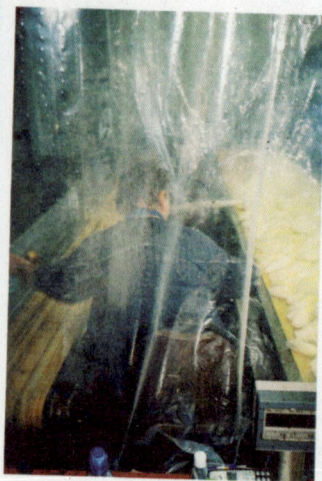

CAT I

Belgïe - Belgique
N° reg. nr.: 32149

Afwijkingsnr.:
N° de dérogation:

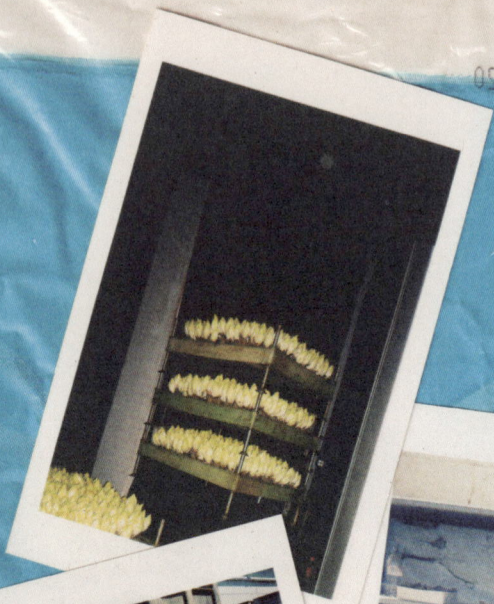

bakker
zakken
huren

etables

"Het komt van de witloofkot hé "

27 dagen
om witloof in het
donker te laten groeien

La bue
le chicon pourri

CHICOREE ★ WITLOOF · ENDIVE · CHICOREE ★ WITLOOF · END

BELORTA
Mechelse Veilingen & Cobra
RTA
BELORTA
Cobra

WITLOOF

ENDIBIA **INDIVIA**

ENDIVE

SOMS DROOM IK
VAN WITLOOF!

WITLOOF

ENDIBIA **INDIVIA**

IVE

SOMS DROOM IK
VAN WITLOOF

The *witloofkot* is the place where the chicory crop is cleaned in preparation of its commodification through international export. The *witloofkot* in Kampenhout in rural Belgium is a place where mostly women work and, consequently, talk. At a simple table turned into a conveyor belt, older Belgian women are joined by Thai women who are newcomers to Belgium. Pia Jacques's conversations with Nook, one of her colleagues at the farm, inspired in her the idea of sending a chicory plant to Nook's hometown so she could show her family in Thailand this 'typically Belgian vegetable'.

A range of administrative, technical and customary regulations made it impossible to send the plant and revealed the absurdities of regulation in the cross-border movements of human workers versus plants. In her contribution, Pia Jacques reminisces on her time at the chicory farm in a series of associative collages that gather analogue pictures taken during her stay, fragmented thoughts and samples of transport materials.

Sometimes I Dream of Chicory

ONE WEEK IN VEYRIER
BY CLAIRE

1 greenhouse
6 ha of soilless cherry tomato crops
harvest starts in January, ends in October
15 staff year-round
50–55 staff during the climax of harvest season
    (April–August)
office hours 7:00 – 12:00, 13:00 – 17:00
    + 15 min. break in the morning and in the
    afternoon
1,000 plants/row
125 m/row
3 blocks, divided into 'chapels'
block 1: 12 chapels, only north side
block 2: 14 chapels, north and south
block 3: 12 chapels, north and south
each chapel is framed by poles
between two poles, there are 5 rows
$(12 \times 5,000) + (14 \times 5,000) \times 2 + (12 \times 5,000) \times 2$
$60,000 + 140,000 + 120,000$
320,000 tomato plants
by the end of October, every plant will be around
    13 m long
$13 \text{ m} \times 320,000 = 4,160,000 \text{ m}$
4,160 km in 6 ha
those plants and the people working in this
    greenhouse produce 25 % of the Swiss
    consumption of cherry tomatoes

Rhythms

PICKING SONG

Piosenka Zbieraczy
Culegerea Cântecului

Mona Thijs

I may be crazy [1]
to push   sto dat
            Sus, sus [2]
                       wracać tam, gdzie byłem już
I may be crazy,   czas
but   hai mișcă-te pentru mine
           mișcă-te pentru mine
           mișcă-te pentru mine
Say, mountain mama [3]
            Cum ești tu cu mine
Say,   Balcani Balcani
                       Jak rozpoznać ludzi,
                       których już nie znamy? [4]
Come on now,   Warszawski dzien
                       pamiętasz
                       kiedy pierwszy raz
                       mnie pokochałeś?

                    w mej głowie [5]
there is an empty road
tell the driver to throttle up
          Sus, sus
do you hear   śpiew czujne jak ptak [6]
                    to są moje marzenia
I belong   to dni, których jeszcze
                    nie znamy
Say, mountain mama
          Cum eşti tu cu mine
Say,   Balcani Balcani
                    Jak rozpoznać ludzi,
                    których już nie znamy? [7]
Come on now,   Warszawski dzien
                    pamiętasz
                    kiedy pierwszy raz
                    mnie pokochałeś? [8]

NOTES

1

Ibrahim, from Bulgaria, chose *Shape of You* by
Ed Sheeran as his favourite picking song. With
one lazy eye he seemed to be staring in the
distance while saying: I don't have any dreams.
What's the point of dreaming if they won't
come true?

2

The Bulgarian-Romanian party song *Turbulence*
by Emilia, Florin Salam and Costi was selected
by Sinan Ali from Bulgaria. He performs as a drum-
mer at Bulgarian wedding parties and came to
Haspengouw to earn money for a hunting gun.

3

Take Me Home, Country Roads by John Denver
was proposed by Jacob, who is Polish. He finds
his own relationship with Poland too complex to
call it home. For him, Max, his labrador, represents "home".

4

Sen o Warszawie by Czesław Niemen is the hymn
of football team Legia Warszawa. Marsin, from
Poland, is one of their fans and he roars the song
before every match. He considers *Sen o Warszawie*
an ode to traditional Poland and "real" Polish
men. He didn't manage to define what a "real"
Polish man should be more precisely.

5

List do m means "Letter to Mum". While picking pears on a field in Haspengouw, Tomek, from Poland, received a call from his brother to say their mother had passed away. *Spadl mi kamien z serca,* he said when he heard the news. By this he meant that a burden had been lifted from his shoulders, since his mother had suffered a lot of pain. The literal translation of *Spadl mi kamien z serca* is: A stone fell from my heart.

6

Jolka Jolka by the Polish band Budka Suflera is a popular love song dedicated to a certain Jolka. Many workers looked up from their phones when this song blared over the speakers. David, the man who requested the song, lowered his eyes.

7

It took a while to convince David, a young Pole, to entrust us with a song. During the first five minutes he laughed away every question and fiddled with his can of energy drink. When it was less crowded, he finally whispered his picking song: *Dni ktorych nie znamy* by Marek Grechuta.

8

Lubie Wracac tam Gdzie Byłem, sung by Zbigniew Wlodecki, means "I want to go back to where I was before". I forgot to note which seasonal worker shared the song, but want to dedicate it to the whole community.

Picking Song is a multilingual song lyric that requires the diverse picking community of Haspengouw to be sung in its entirety. It builds on Mona Thijs's radio series *Playlist of de Pluk* (2022), in which she asked several seasonal workers to share a song that is meaningful to them during the picking period and to contribute to a collaborative picking playlist. The radio series explored the tension between multilingualism and music within the picking community in Haspengouw. In the song text produced, Mona combines the lyrics of these picking songs into a new song text that inverts and samples the original meanings of the lyrics into a new multilingual whole. In the margins of this new picking song, footnotes have been added, hinting at some of the personal stories behind the chosen songs. *Picking Song* is a symbol of both the complexities and opportunities of multilingualism within the picking community.

English translation:

I may be crazy
to push a hundred dates
Up, up
to where I was before
I may be crazy,
but come on, time, move for me
move for me
move for me

Say, mountain mama
How am I doing?
Say, Balkan Balkan
How do you recognize people you don't know anymore?
Come on now, Warsaw day
do you remember
when you first loved me?

In my head there is an empty road
tell the driver to throttle up
Up, up
Do you hear the singing, agile as a bird
these are my dreams
I belong to days that are to come

Say, mountain mama
How am I doing?
Say, Balkan Balkan
How do you recognize people you don't know anymore?
Come on now, Warsaw day
do you remember
when you first loved me?

FIVE DAYS IN A GREENHOUSE

Intensive Organic Farming

Claire Chassot

August 2020.
I arrived in the morning.
I don't remember what time it was,
but I was on time.

I parked my car next to the others, entered the
shed, changed in the women's locker room, left
my things on the bench, passed the gate where
soles and hands are disinfected, walked past the
metallic and repetitive noise of the packaging line,
the shrill alarms of the robots pulling carts filled
with crates of empty trays. Then I entered the
greenhouse.

Six hectares.

Rows of tomatoes everywhere. Plants that stretch
to the top of the greenhouse, soilless. Plants that
seem to have no visible roots.

The soil is covered in plastic, the tomatoes float one
metre above it. They grow on thick, gnarled vines,
dark-green and cream-streaked. Monstrous plants
supported by metal hooks one metre off the ground.
Behind these piles of horizontal vines, more bundles of horizontal vines.

320,000 feet, but where are they anchored? Where
are their roots? What makes this jungle of tomato
plants grow?

Each plant rises upright, wrapped around a thin rope, its head so close to the glass and the sun that workers have to watch them daily to turn them over when they are in danger of burning. Up there, the workers wear sun hats. Below, I see only the bare vines, hanging, their roots camouflaged. I stay still, in the middle of the central aisle, my pupils constricted by the light, trying to make sense of the sounds and movements around me. I don't know if the heat is knocking me out or if the rhythm in this space has been slowed down.

Finally, the foreman calls out to me. He tells me how to wear my gloves. How to disinfect the clippers every 20 m. How to cut the leaves so the sun can reach the fruit. I enter one of the lines. Suddenly, silence. No one is visible anymore, except for the plants. I cut. 150 metres to the right, 150 to the left. You have to let the leaves fall on the ground, not on the vines. It is hot, humid, quiet. I forget to drink. I didn't bring a water bottle. I'm hypnotized by my own gestures, green everywhere, the heat, the silence.

Each worker is alone in their aisle. Each worker has 150 metres to themselves, with a screen of greenery on each side. If I work, I will only see tomato plants and bumblebees. By the end of the first day, I have talked to one worker only. She worried about my lack of water and the risk of dehydration. If I want to get anything out of this week other than the awareness of my lack of expe-

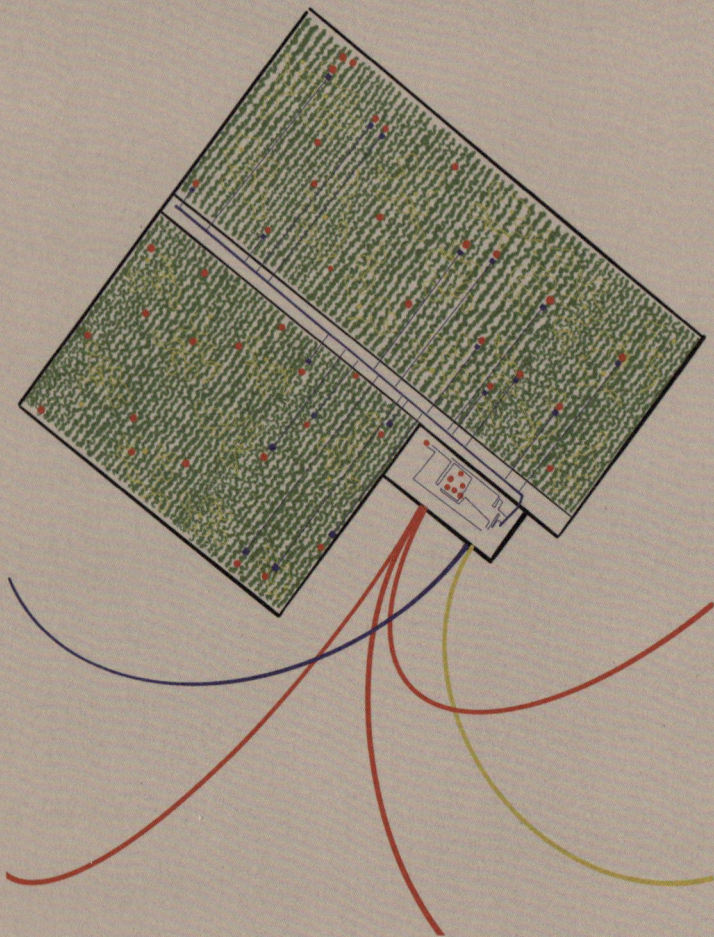

Five Days in a Greenhouse

rience, I need to ask questions. To ask questions, I need to accompany other workers, not become one.

On the second day, I accompany the person in charge of bio control. On the third, the one in charge of workers. On the fourth, I pick tomatoes for a day. On the last day, I film, photograph, observe. By the end of the week, I have a number of movements, gestures and links in mind that all revolve around these 320,000 tomato plants and their fruit production. The greenhouse is a vortex where everything is coordinated to produce a quarter of all cherry tomatoes in Switzerland.

In November and December, the greenhouse is emptied, cleaned, disinfected and prepared for next year's crops.

In January the tomato plants are planted in substrate. The harvest starts soon after. Each passing month yields more tomatoes, as the plants grow throughout their ten-month existence. At the end of the season, the longest stems will be thirteen metres. Their growth is an imperceptible movement to the eye. The plants gradually fill the space, the entire height, the entire length.

In August, when I arrive, the greenhouse is entirely green and the perspective monotonous. The aisles stretch and repeat themselves. At the back, opaque glass walls seem unreachable. The eye searches for focus points: the red tomatoes, the soil covered in white, a yellow line in the central aisle. It's by raising our heads, by following a vine, that we finally find an exit. The glass roof panels are transparent, open to the sky. The tomato stems are wound around a (biodegradable) rope, suspended from a cable by an S-shaped hook. The cable is stretched, horizontally, almost to the top of the greenhouse, just before the spot where the sun would burn the leaves.

Some of the workers – exclusively men, I am told – stand on lifting platforms, at the level of the cables. They monitor the growth of the plants daily to bring them down when they become too big. They are called the turners. Their gestures maintain an altitude that is not to be exceeded. They monitor the internal horizon of the greenhouse. They bring the plants down. At the bottom, one metre off the floor, the feet are suspended horizontally so as not to drag on the ground. It is between these two horizons that the gigantism is perceived. In August, the plants have been growing for seven months, trying to reach the top of the greenhouse, the sky, the light. During the first four months, their growth has been accompanied, supported by ropes. Then the ropes are gone and the turners begin to thwart their ascent, to make them fall back down with each new sucker. With each turn of the hook, the heads are moved about twenty centimetres to the left. They slide horizontally now, sometimes changing row,

Rhythms

moving away from their roots, experimenting a crab-like movement. Tirelessly they seek verticality, tirelessly the turners impose this lateral movement on them, this slight shift maintaining the hope of reaching the top while at the same time preventing it. The turners' gestures create diagonals to hold the plants between these parallel horizons.

I try to understand their gesture and its consequences.

This is one of the rare gestures constraining the movement of the plants. It was designed to contain their growth without interrupting it, but more importantly to facilitate the gestures of the other workers. By keeping the head at this height, the ripe tomatoes are always between 1.45 m and 1.60 m above ground level, and so are the leaves to be cut. This way, the cutters and pickers work at a constant and ergonomic height.

The cutters clip some of the foliage off at the level of the reddening tomatoes so the plant has more energy to dedicate to fruit and more direct light. These are the movements I learned on the first day. At the beginning of each row, a pair of clippers and a spray bottle of bleach to clean the blade every twenty metres. Each plant has to be pruned to start the transformation of the bushy plant into a bare vine, because soon, once the tomatoes are picked, the vertical part will become horizontal, interlacing with the other vines. The gesture is simple, the

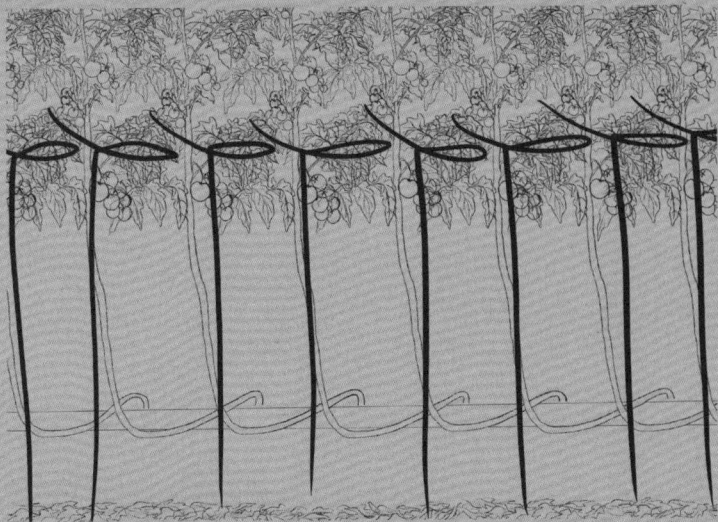

Rhythms

crucial issue is the number of leaves to remove. Some above the tomatoes, every single one below.

At the same height, but in different rows, the pickers harvest the bunches and fill the trays. These are exclusively female gestures. The manager of the greenhouse explained to me that women are, from experience, more delicate and therefore make better pickers. This is what I do on the fourth day. Every step counts, starting with how to stack the empty boxes on the cart. The foreman gives me a demonstration.

The goal of these manipulations is to carry only empty crates. I'm impressed but don't remember the sequence and spend some time in the middle of my aisle trying to figure out how not to carry one of the crates I've filled. I'm much slower than the other pickers anyway and I'm putting too many cherry tomatoes in the trays. This will slow down the workers at the packing line. The work of the pickers is closely linked to those working in the packing hangar. They master each gesture perfectly. One hand holding the bunch while the other cuts the stem close to the vine. A quarter turn to the left to put the bunch in a tray. And already the hand is holding the next bunch. They do not hesitate about the level of maturity of the fruit, nor about the number of bunches to put in a tray, and even less about the movement of the crates. They move along the row almost without stopping, their cart always in motion, their chest rotating. A quarter turn to the right towards the plants, a quarter turn to the left towards the crates, one step forward, a loop at the end of the line to start again.

In one row, sometimes less, the twenty-four boxes on the cart are full and sent back to the central aisle. There, robots take over. A small yellow robot pulls the carts to the shed. It follows a yellow line which guides it from one end of the six hectares to the other. It pulls up to ten carts behind it. Once it's at the right dock, a robotic system collects the full crates, weighs them and sends them on a conveyor belt to another robot that stacks the boxes on pallets to be taken to the cold room. The robot that drives the carts does not leave immediately. It waits for another robot system involving arms, conveyor belts, etc. to unfold new crates, put empty plastic trays in them and place twenty-four crates on each cart. Only then does it go back to the greenhouse. There, the pickers take a cart each and continue their work.

At the entrance of each row, they have to clock in. And each cart is weighed when it arrives in the hangar. This way, the employers can see who has filled which one and get an idea of the productivity of each picker. This doesn't stop the breaks at the back of the lines, the tomato tastings and the stash of bunches in the sleeves of jackets. I found it stashing, entering the greenhouse with a jacket on the arm. It's when I finally reached the end of my 150 metres of picking that I understood the value of this accessory. It serves as a basket. At the end of the day, the jackets camouflage a few bunches of tomatoes and almost nobody helps themselves to the self-service trays at the exit of the sheds. Tomatoes taste better when you pick them yourself. And these jacket tomatoes are ultimately the only ones that will be carried by humans in this greenhouse. They are nestled in the crooks of arms, hidden in the folds of fabric and held in hands whereas the others, the official bunches, are rushed from plant to tray. Barely touched before being handed over to the robots.

I need some time, the whole fifth day, to observe this chain of robots and untangle their different functions, the different noises. What is an alarm and what is just the sound of a machine running? The hangar contrasts loudly with the greenhouse. On a few square metres, all this mechanical and electronic machinery unloads, weighs, packs, labels and stacks tons of cherry tomatoes every day. As much as the greenhouse slowed down my gestures because of the heat and silence, this hangar makes me focus on the noise and micro-gestures accomplished simultaneously. Here, the flows are dictated by the outside, the comings and goings of the trucks on the loading dock. The tomatoes are invisible, in the cold room, waiting to be desired. In the greenhouse, everything revolves around the plant. I see it in contrast to this space.

Rhythms

All the machinery, all the architecture of the green-house is designed to serve the tomatoes. Pipes provide the right amount of each nutrient for optimal growth. Other pipes diffuse water vapour to maintain the right level of humidity. Another one diffuses CO_2 because there is not enough inside the greenhouse. The substrate fulfils its role of mechanical support and for the transfer of nutrients to the roots.

Hives of bumblebees are delivered weekly to pollinate the flowers. Auxiliary insects are ordered on a regular basis to control the pests observed on the yellow sticky strips. All these insects come from the Netherlands. Pheromone traps are set randomly to disrupt pest reproduction. Everything that enters the greenhouse is at the service of these giant plants, their health and productivity. They themselves serve a huge consumption of cherry tomatoes in all seasons. These six hectares provide 25 % of annual consumption in Switzerland.

Only the sun does not play along this game of consistency. Because artificial lighting is forbidden, the greenhouse still depends on the sun, on its cycle and on a nearby mountain, east of the greenhouse, which delays its rising every day. A mountain close enough to make the greenhouse, its rhythms and gestures, stop for two months every year. The extreme care devoted to these plants during ten months led me to question what becomes of them.

What happens to the 320,000 tomato plants after they are uprooted? Could we imagine gestures to prolong our collaboration with these plants, to value them beyond their fruits? And what would they be? I think about the gestures of basketry to extend their use, to turn productive plants into receiving ones.

* Names in this text are pseudonyms.

ONE WEEK IN AINET
BY ANASTASIA

802 km from home
4 hrs 28 min. on the train, 1 hr 11 min. on the train, 34 min. on the train
1 hr 24 min. on the bus
21 min. wait at the bus stop

day 1: rain until late morning, haying postponed, watering balcony geraniums

day 2: rain until early morning, haying postponed, watering balcony geraniums, minor garden work

day 3: no rain in the morning, showers in the early afternoon, haying postponed, watering balcony geraniums, weeding the garden, minor cleaning tasks, walk to the neighbours' with farmer's mother (showers on the way back)

day 4: rain during the night, haying postponed, drive up to the hut, looking for cows and feeding them with farmer's father, rain again when coming back from cows

day 5: rain during the night, haying postponed, drive back to farm, watering balcony geraniums

day 6: rain in the morning, haying postponed, watering balcony geraniums, ironing, gathering herbs with farmer's mother

day 7: no rain, church holiday, farmer at the church

day 8: departure, still watering balcony geraniums, rain starts again in the afternoon

SEEDING NOISE

A Concert for Strawberries (sketches & scores)

Caroline Profanter and Ines Marita Schärer

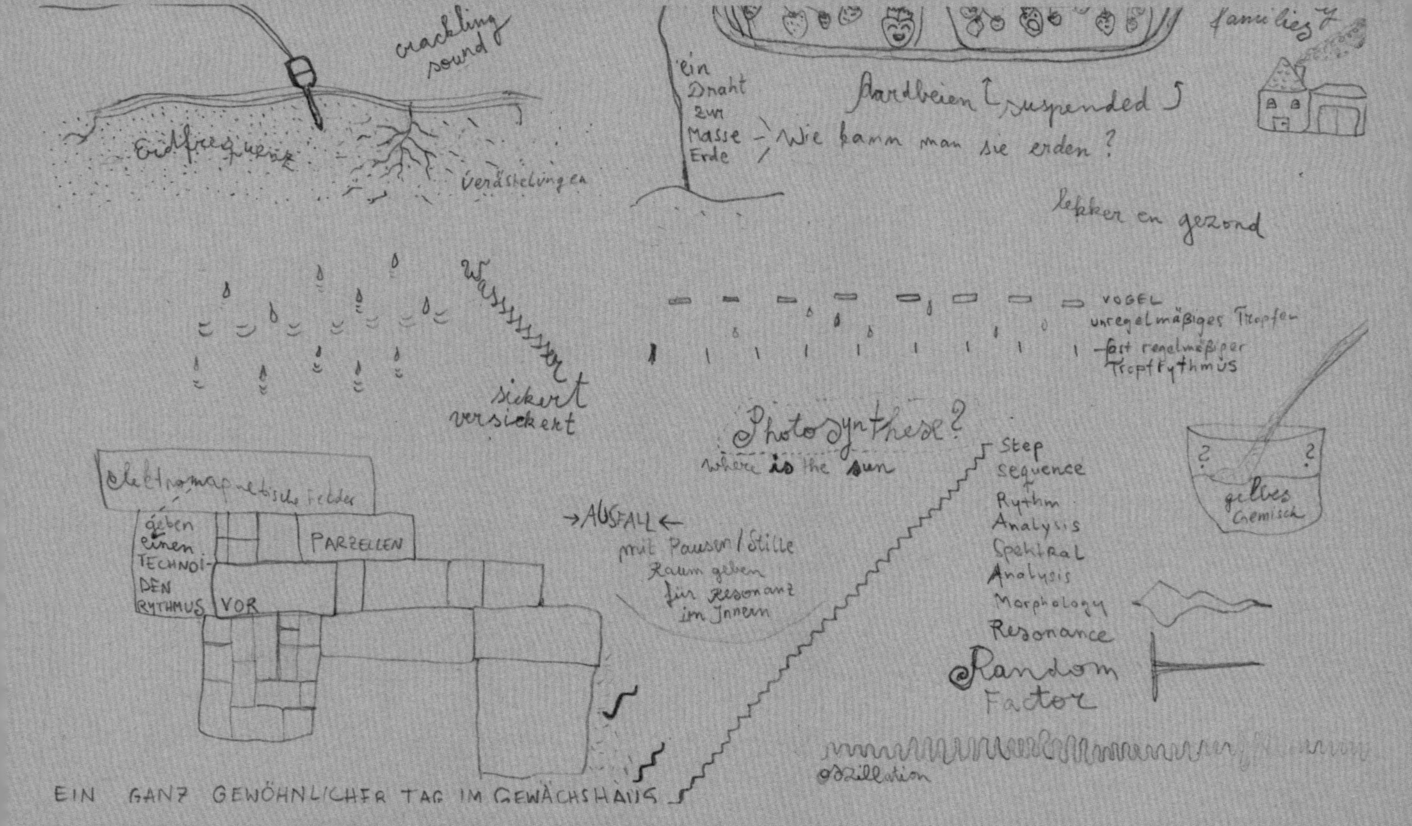
crackling sound
Erdfrequenz
Verästelungen
ein Draht zur Masse Erde
Aardbeien [suspended]
Wie kann man sie erden?
families
lekker en gezond
Wasssssser
sickert
versickert
VOGEL
unregelmäßiges Tropfen
fast regelmäßiger Tropfrythmus
Photosynthese?
where is the sun
elektromagnetische Felder
geben einen TECHNOI-DEN RYTHMUS VOR
PARZELLEN
→AUSFALL←
mit Pausen/Stille Raum geben für Resonanz im Innern
Step sequence
Rythm Analysis
Spektral Analysis
Morphology
Resonance
Random Factor
gelbes Gemisch
oszillation
EIN GANZ GEWÖHNLICHER TAG IM GEWÄCHSHAUS

Silent soils ◄

mean JJ% interval

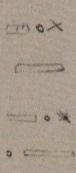

ⁱ ⁱ □ □ ˣ
at different speeds

1 plant → 100 flowers
KASKADIERUNG
1^{100}

Scheinfrucht
sweet
seduction

Überfluss
Ultra Red

interaction workers plants
Atm. , Wind Glass
CO_2? Glass

3 Spuren   Result like a plant   VEGETAL LIFE

electromagnetic strawberry fields

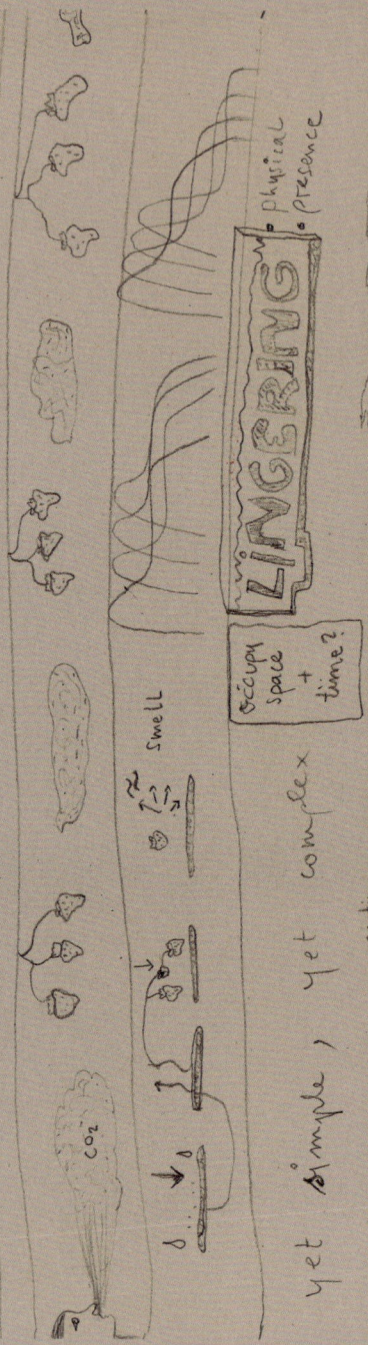

CO_2

Smell

LINGERING — Physical Presence

occupy space + time?

yet simple, yet complex

ARBEIT

SUN

time   0

Byproduct

shape

seeds
dropping
a
pulse
becomes
texture

FIELDS

Osterzufall?
ERDBEERE
AARDBEIE
FRAGOLA
FRAISE
FRESA

QUALITY : A

ORIGIN : ... ...

Daily rituals
a noise
happened

it just continues
every day

noise happens
every day

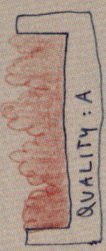

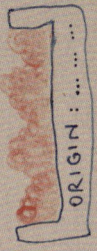

SYNTHESIS

RADIO

frequency
modulated

A red
just white
and then yellow
maybe green
fruit
could it become blue?
Can we communicate?
only through others
☐ give water   ☐ dance
☐ make shadow   ☐ do improvise

hole in the
whole atmosphere
containers
of seeds
of dots
of branches
like strings
shaking

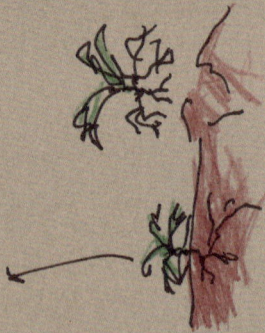

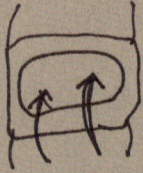

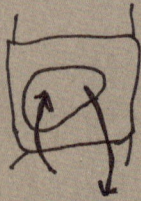

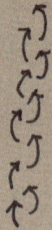

Push!
Squeeze

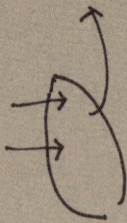

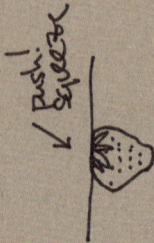

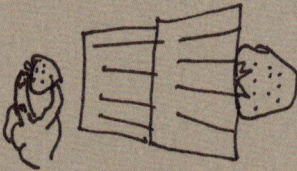

strong
stronger

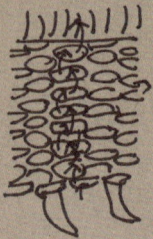

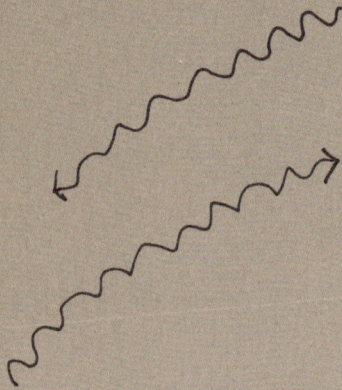

Bumblebee
Drone

mute
silence

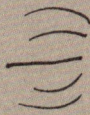

glowing

temporidity

multitemporalities

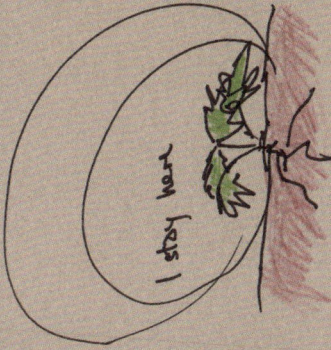

I stay hear

watering

biggas

estud
recai !

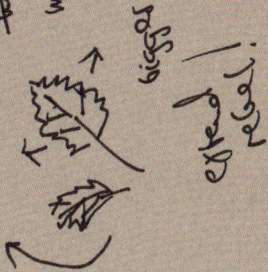

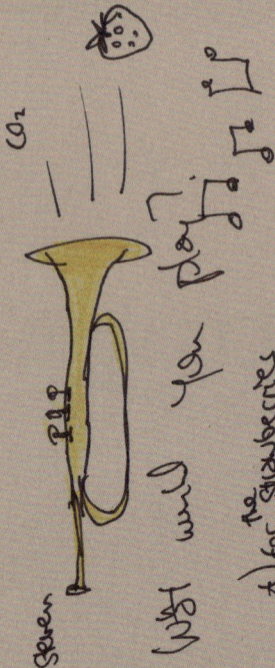

Seven CO_2

What will you playing

A) for the strawberries
is) for the warriors

2.

dance up and down

wash
morning
evening

Nake?

"your vibration is you currency"

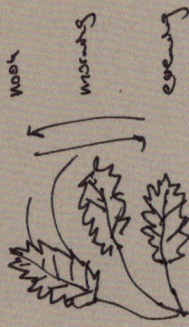

Trembling?   Dancing

Breath
Pusation
Beating

vibrating

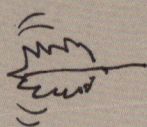

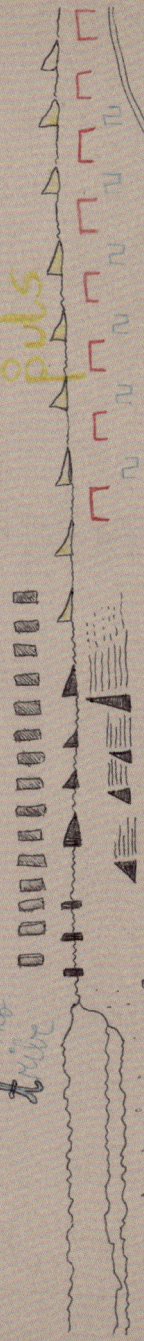
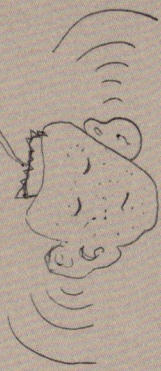
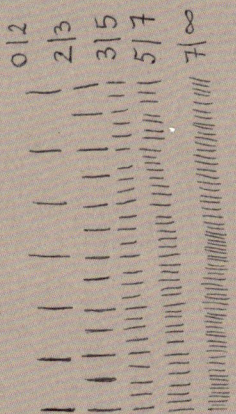
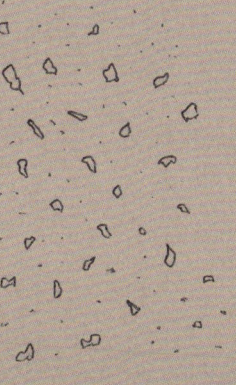

mono

Spielköpfe

pots

0 2
2 3
3 5
5 7
7 8

das Pepern soll weg

bei 12:30

send & receive

skip bars
~ 14 - 17 mm

machine
missions
everywhere

running

"apply the same
Sounds to all channels
more often"

was ist im gelben schein

repeat ethan
memorable
sein in
w. the loop

surfaces → atmosphere

alle 6
Sekunden
ein schwarer

humidity
light
electric discharge von

voices
Radonaurus
$H_2O + CO_2 + heat$
Juvalten

Tropfen

bruelet
sich
aus
über das
gorite
Feld
⇒ Plane

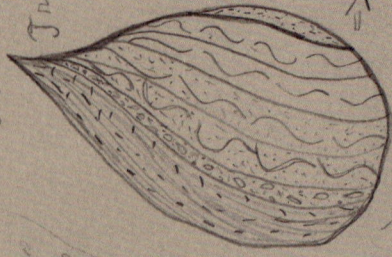

A-
Zusammenspiel / SYNCHRONIZITÄT

"Eythm is a Dancer" Loop
[Stimme + Sona flecher] [Nitrogeneusia]
Impulsgenerator
Rauscher
(MAX AUDIOTESTER)   6000ms > release 4000ms

Incidence Incidenzen aus der Klangspur: Rohr rain 0056.wav

in phase / out of phase

[Wahrphase]
↓
[Ludg?]

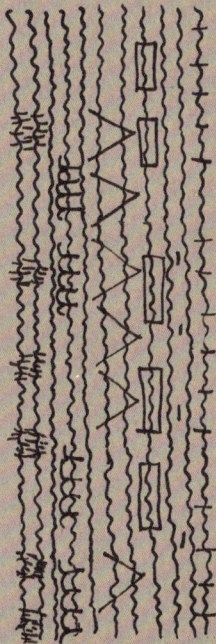

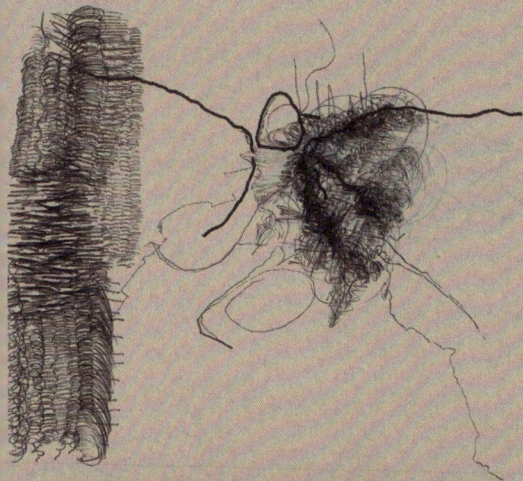

While engaging with the context of a strawberry greenhouse, Ines Marita Schärer and composer Caroline Profanter became fascinated by the opposing forces of the technological sounds heard in the field and the greenhouse and by the natural biodynamic rhythms due to their own movement. Their work shifts our focus away from the human towards the more-than-human entities in agriculture, namely, strawberries. By listening, they highlight the small modes of natural resistance within this disciplined and highly organized production environment. Shifting between sonic sensations of human, mechanical and more-than-human beings, the work translates sounds into speculative ideas, images, drawings and scores. The images selected here include a set of drawings that functioned as scores as well as playful retranslations within the artistic process of listening, recording, composing and producing sound.

STAYING CLOSE: VALUES OF WORKING THE LAND

Conversation with Fernando García-Dory from Inland

Claire Chassot, Anastasia Eggers
and Maximiliaan Royakkers

While Seasonal Neighbours participated in the agricultural and horticultural contexts of Western Europe, Inland was initiated in response to the rural exodus taking place in Northern Spain. First involved in different localities, they now think and develop their practices from a single village in the Spanish countryside by working together with local rural practices. Inland's experience of working the land presents several differences by comparison with ours, one being the value attributed to the skills of workers. During our conversation with Inland's founder Fernando García-Dory, we explored and questioned farming work, workers, their values and the possibilities that the links between cultural and agricultural systems can bring to help develop more durable relationships with our environment, labour and seasonality in a wide sense.

> SN: Before introducing us to the work of Inland, we are curious to know whether you have encountered or engaged with forms of seasonal work in your practice? Could you describe practices that come to mind when thinking about seasonal forms of agricultural labour?

IL: What comes to mind are the travelling companies of sheep shearers, which is a seasonal phenomenon. Most of the workers from this sector come from Eastern Europe or sometimes from Paraguay and Uruguay because their season starts in summer, which is winter in Europe, after which they come here during the European summer. There are also the workers that participate in the summer pasture. In our Shepherds' School, we train young shepherds that are hired for the summer on the mountain pastures, *alpage* in French, *Alm* in German. The shearers are often very much in demand, they are in a kind of prominent position because there are not that many people who accept shearing jobs. These examples are very different from what would be the exploitative model of farm labour which you, as the Seasonal Neighbours collective, engaged in, or the illegal migration taking place in Southern European contexts.

Can you explain to us how Inland
started and describe what you do today?

Inland's involvement with rural localities evolved from introducing it as a field of analysis and tentative approach into operating within it as a practice. Over the course of our fifteen years of existence, we started introducing the rural question by organizing an international conference and twenty-two artist residencies in twenty-two villages. This first attempt to engage progressively developed into a way of working that we call a durational community of practices. Today we are restoring an abandoned village in the Spanish countryside and also run the Centre for the Approach of the Rural – CAR in Madrid.[1] Both spaces host a programme, engage with the surrounding context and receive practitioners that join our activities. We also participate in biennales and other artistic events. In the village, we take part in rural activities like producing dairy and cheese; we have a flock of about a hundred sheep and twenty goats and are currently discussing with other colleagues the transformation of a eucalyptus plantation into an autochthonous forest that could launch the production of oils and mushrooms. It's also from here that we run the Shepherd School and facilitate the European Shepherds Network. So in this locality, we are in close contact with what could be the conversion of our farming sector.

> How has this evolution in your involvement with different rural contexts changed the way you work as a collective of art professionals, farmers and villagers?

First of all I would say that Inland is more a project or the idea of a project about an organization, or a para-institution. The social form that our platform of collaborations takes has been evolving. When I started, I was working on my own, supported by a team to develop different aspects of the project, such as communication and finances. At one point this way of working evolved into another collabo-

1   Inland.org, https://car.inland.org

rative form, with others joining to develop specific elements. The risk with this way of working is that the collective, and the people working in the team, end up in a structure and place of pure cultural production, which creates a growing distance from the practices on the land. That is one of the things we are trying in the village, to stay close to the land and its practices.

In fact, rather than working as a collective, the model we work in is that of a village. In contrast to collectives, which are sometimes based on ideas according to which everybody has to share the same level of knowledge and agency, the village operates more as a set of individual activities that gather for communal aspects.

In our day-to-day activities, we take care of the animals here in the village, we build and farm, and there are also cultural operations like this interview or the preparation of exhibitions because we get invitations to do projects: for example, this year Manifesta (in Barcelona), the Lahore Biennale (in Pakistan) and Colomboscope (in Sri Lanka). As the level of internal friction that the dynamics of the art world are generating in our local project is growing, I think Inland could favour the transition from a cultural model very much based on the way the 1990s and early 2000s global contemporary art market worked and start to slow down. We need to question hyperproductivity, hypermobility, the idea of the nomadic global player.

What we often notice through our work is the gap between a romanticized understanding of the land and its reality today. Every year about a hundred people apply for our Shepherds School programme to become a shepherd and often the motivations behind applications are a sort of yearning for the idealized notion of pastoralism that is at odds with what it actually entails.

> It is interesting that you mention this gap and a growing disconnect from the land. Throughout our personal fieldwork in different industrial horticultural farms, we have experienced that this disconnect is also growing in the farms themselves. This poses questions about notions of locality and how embedded farming practices still are. We could raise similar concerns about artistic practices that engage with the rural.

It is very important for us that people who are engaged in the team, the collective, share everyday farming activities. What happens too often in our cultural sectors is that artists or cultural producers develop ideas and talk on behalf of other subjects. In our case, the problem we want to face is the lack of articulation of the everyday by the farmers themselves. If we were to reproduce that form of, say, extractivism or even impose a certain form of voice, we would be reproducing what we want to question in the first place. The *peintres de plein air*, for example, went to the countryside to capture the instant, picturesque beauty of the milkmaid but they were not at all willing to milk a cow themselves. This raises questions when thinking about the fact that this image and representation was later consumed by the bourgeois market of the nineteenth century who at the same time were industrializing and progressively evicting small producers from the land.

I think our goal is to understand the community of inhabitants in the place we are and that of course can't happen through a collective. Because we hardly see this idea of collective in the countryside, I am starting to think that the idealization of the collective as a collaborative form comes from the lack of other forms of exchange and community that people have in cities. If I had to define the collective aspect of Inland, I would rather use the form of implicit communal thinking of shepherds living together in the summer pastures practising mutual support and sharing activities while holding onto aspects of their individualities.

As industrial farming evolves towards the greater technologization and even robotization of farm work, turning the farmer into an operator in a control room, depriving us from what actually working the land or with animals involves, this is something that I think every farmer has to ask themselves and stay alert to. But this applies to almost every domain of life today. Is technology preventing us from actually *living*, under the promise of freeing up time for life? Especially in farming, higher technologization leads to increasing dependence and subordination to the companies providing those means.

> You mentioned that you are not only
> involved in the village and in the
> centre in Madrid, but that you also try
> to connect cultural contexts to rural
> communities through interventions in
> art manifestations like biennales.
> How do you operate in those contexts?

Since our contribution to the Istanbul Biennial in 2013, I realized that in order to carry out a project in a context like that, what would make sense is not to bring an idea and develop it but to understand what the local ally that we want to contact is doing and how we could establish a dialogue connecting both our practices to start an exchange. For example, at the last Istanbul Biennial we were working with a community of producers in a village in Kars in the North of Turkey, on the border with Armenia. We learned that they were working with interesting economic models for tourism and cheese production and that they were interested in engaging with wool. As we had been working with wool for some time, we had the opportunity to start a dialogue between what they do and what we do. In the end we were involved in the exhibition making to an equal degree. They were present at the Biennial; afterwards they were commissioned by an alternative coop restaurant to have their wool cushions made by the association in the village. I think that it's about finding who in those contexts is doing work that relates to what we are doing and then creating a form of fixing that is more horizontal rather than have Inland turn up with an idea and try to implement it without knowing much about the context.

To facilitate this dynamic, collaborating with a host structure that is active in the communities we want to connect with is essential. I don't think an artist can just come and go and produce something relevant, unless there is a host structure that guarantees that there is both a prior process and an after process. With formats like a commission in a biennial that has to have a certain spectacular visualization, we have to carefully negotiate the rhythms and temporalities of the different processes we take part in. We rely very much on local anchoring organizations to help us in this, and also to ensure that our presence is not crucial, that there is an ongoing force that continues without us. Because in the end the emphasis of our projects is always on developing practices on the land.

> In those shorter-term engagements and links between biennales, institutions, cultural sectors and rural communities, have you managed to

set up collaborations that are durable
over time, similar to your engagement
in the village?

I should think case by case, but it doesn't always
work. One example could be the project *Lament of
the Newt* that I made for the Gwangju Biennale in
South Korea.[2] I spent a year working with a local
community on creating a theatre company to protect a piece of land from development and then I
left and I didn't stay in touch with them, which of
course was very difficult because I had to work
with translators and so on. Overall, I think that the
networks and the projects we keep more in contact
with and that we continue to exchange with are
the ones that are part of the social movements and
networks that we tried to set up. For example, in
the case of our participation in Documenta 15, the
lumbung practice introduced by ruangrupa was a
concept of collective exchange and we developed
one of the working groups which would become
the lumbung land group in which we are now trying to keep those exchanges alive.[3] Another example
would be the World Alliance of Mobile Indigenous
Peoples (WAMIP) or the Confederacy of Villages

2   "Agro-Ecology, Collectivity and the Post-Pastoral: An Interview with Fernando
      García-Dory," Carolina Ramos, *Berlin Art Link,* May 22, 2020, https://www.
      berlinartlink.com/2020/05/22/agro-ecology-and-new-pastoralism-an-inter-
      view-with-fernando-garcia-dory/.
3   "Where Art is Fertile. The lumbung Interlokal and Other Forms of Shaking the
      Land," Fernando García-Dory, *Arts of the Working Class,* October 10, 2023,
      https://artsoftheworkingclass.org/text/where-art-is-fertile.

(CONV),[4] a European network of artist spaces in rural areas. These are examples in which we really became a partner and in which we continue investing time and energy.

Of course, it takes a lot of time to create and develop these relationships. Finding support for and sustaining the person that is dedicated to facilitating the network is a process of militant work. There are various difficulties, as it mostly depends on social funding and applications. We try to counter this by transitioning to a more reliant economy based on our own productions.

> In these exchanges between art
> systems and rural systems, can we
> still think about an audience?
> Or a public outside of those systems
> that you address?

Our primary audiences are the participants and communities we work with. Of course this first form of public is complemented with moments of sharing and exchange in other contexts. This was the idea from the start with Inland. In the beginning we were working in villages around the country producing art projects that then would be presented both in Madrid in an art context as well as in the villages themselves. I think that there is a

4   "Confederacy of Villages," https://www.confederacyofvillages.org and "WAMIP. World Alliance of Mobile Indigenous Peoples," http://wamipglobal.com.

moment of extending what has happened primarily in the process of activation and creation that is also very important to us. In the more classic formats of contemporary art, one shares a transient moment of exchange with somebody that comes to check or look and tries to understand something. These audiences are not necessarily so engaged with the context as a local audience. Still, sharing the work in those spaces can have a strong effect. When we created an artwork with a dairy farmer in the UK, and later presented the project in the context of Frieze Art in London, the effect of endorsing and reaffirming the dairy farmer's expression was very strong. That's why to me there have to be different levels of creation and sharing with different audiences.

Was it easy to engage people from rural areas in these art manifestations?

No! It is long-term work. You need to find the right interests, you have to connect with an existing need and identify a pleasure that the people you are collaborating with can obtain. But in the end, that's the thing; how can culture and art be part of everyday life, not just something that is made by professionals for museums and the market? There is a level of activation that you only start to see as a possibility when you are embedded in a local context and its community, and that is something that takes time.

III

Rituals

SEASONAL RITUALS IN A POST-SEASONAL WORLD

A Farmers' Almanac for the New Rural

Anastasia Eggers

Our sense of seasonality is rooted in the traditional understanding of the agricultural timeline of the year that is guided by the sun. However, the reality of horticultural production in Western Europe looks different: planting periods are increasingly driven by factors such as market conditions, geopolitical circumstances and labour availability instead of sunlight, rain or other climatic conditions. When our dependence on these 'post-seasonal' cycles is severed due to geopolitical shifts or changes in market conditions, new agricultural dynamics arise, inspiring several members of Seasonal Neighbours.

In this text, Anastasia Eggers reflects on her research on the notions of seasonality and rural rituals. By designing a post-seasonal almanac, she created a narrative that links traditional harvest celebrations with the *in situ* experiments of Seasonal Neighbours members Karolina Michalik and Collectif dallas as well as her own interventions.

POST-SEASONALITY IN DUTCH GREENHOUSE HORTICULTURE

The realization that industrial agriculture is characterized by a concept like 'post-seasonality' only quietly seeped into my mind. It started with my quest for a seasonal job. Assuming that there would be an acute harvest season in greenhouses in summer, I called thirty-six greenhouses in an attempt to find a job in Westland, the horticultural greenhouse complex around the corner from where I lived at that time. Hardly any growers were interested in hiring me as a short-term worker – most of them required a more or less constant flow of work, with some moments of peak season that would be balanced out through workers coming from employment agencies. The farmer who agreed to give me a job for a couple of weeks talked about the possibility of cultivating greenhouse aubergines in Westland all year round.

Greenhouse horticulture is attempting to create conditions and environments that are as detached as possible from the natural environment, with the aim to enhance the 'sun' season – to grow larger quantities and 'better-quality' crops, and to boost, increase and maximize the harvest. Every single factor is controlled, which allows for an almost autarkic food production that is part of the new, post-seasonal world. This type of controlled environment creates conditions that foster efficient plant growth that aims to extend the seasons as much as possible, almost to the point that seasonality is eliminated to ensure an uninterrupted flow of produce – as long as it is still profitable.

When I was following the farmer's brother into the rows of three-metre-long aubergine plants, asking questions about the timing of the season, he told me: 'We have to stop before the Spanish aubergines arrive', referring to week 44, a moment of the year during which the Spanish aubergines replace the Dutch ones on supermarket shelves. With the increasing number of aubergines on the market, prices would drop, and it wouldn't be viable any longer to continue the production, so Dutch growers define it as the moment to stop their harvest. This made me realize that this post-seasonal condition develops new types of dependencies on human-made factors. This in turn triggered the idea to define the notion of a 'post-seasonal' – geopolitical, financial, market-based or labour-oriented – seasonality that influences crops and their natural cycles.

In 2022, for instance, Russia's full-scale invasion of Ukraine resulted in shorter seasons in Dutch greenhouses. Russia's restriction of gas supplies in response to Western sanctions caused an energy crisis in Europe. As gas prices skyrocketed, greenhouse growers weren't able to maintain the length of the season. In particular, growers of energy-intensive crops like tomatoes and cucumbers that rely on gas for both heating and lighting started the season in 2022 a couple of months later and ended much earlier. In post-Brexit UK, visa rules and tax regulations held back the harvest of crops. For example, the new and very promising, ever-bearing strawberry variety called Ace is at risk of not having enough harvesters from Eastern Europe, as its season lasts longer than the workers' income tax allowances.

This kind of narratives made me question how as a society we can navigate this complexity. Despite a growing call for eating seasonally, consumers

4

A collective reflection on energy in times of crisis

PIPELINE STARGAZING

GEOPOLITICAL SEASON

have very little understanding of what this actually means within the current food system. We find ourselves in supermarket aisles surrounded by a never-changing sequence of fruit and vegetables, rarely realizing that the label indicating the origin changes every now and again. The demand and desire for year-round availability of crops generated an uninterrupted season facilitated by global trade in which the understanding of the actual seasons is lost. Moreover, it is crucial to understand the notion of seasonality through the lens of locality.

Greenhouse horticulture creates conditions that are hard to describe as local as they try to detach production from every factor that can be described as such. This includes soil and climate as well as the labour force that at the moment can't be sourced entirely locally. For instance, while asparagus remains one of the vegetables with a more pronounced season in the Netherlands and Germany, it is still being replaced by its Spanish and Peruvian versions, blurring the seasonal boundaries of the locally produced shoots. If locality can be thought of as a limitation, the concept of seasonality would be a tool for giving a rhythm to this limitation and making it a means to relate to the natural world.

SEASONAL CELEBRATIONS

The Ice Saints in Western and Eastern European folklore dictate a widely applied farmers' rule not to plant crops before mid May to prevent frosting. They were adopted in Christianity as the feast days of St Mamertus, St Pancras and St Servatius. Seasonal celebrations mostly relate to natural phenomena that played a role in farming. Often they originate from pre-Christian times and were later adapted to the Christian context, like Christmas, which is thought to have derived from the winter solstice. Some celebrations like Halloween hint at the occurrence of specific natural events that could have been connected to farming but failed to maintain a strong connection.

The sequence of these celebrations used to make up the structure of the agricultural year, highlighting its most crucial moments: in several cultures, the beginning of the agricultural year was marked by festivities connected to fertility and the cyclic awakening of nature after the winter period, which would often manifest itself in burning effigies such as straw dolls on a bonfire.[1] In Belgium, Germany and the north of France as well as Switzerland and Austria, these types of festivities have taken shape as the Carnival that is celebrated on the first Sunday of Lent, a pagan celebration that was later adapted

---

[1]   Alessandro Testa, "Fertility and the Carnival 2: Popular Frazerism and the Reconfiguration of Tradition in Europe Today," *Folklore 128* (June 2017), 112.

into Christianity. The end of winter is followed by the spring equinox, a celebration of the land's fertility turned into Easter, which for example in Germany is still celebrated with an Easter bonfire, the ashes of which would traditionally be mixed with seeds before sowing. This illustrates how actions that needed to be taken to achieve soil fertility would be ritualized.

The spring equinox is followed by moments of care and protection of the crops: next to the Ice Saints, in Alpine regions, the Night of Cold Sophie is marked by lighting fires to protect existing crops. In some countries, midsummer celebrations are connected to predictions about the productivity of crops and fires lit up for the celebrations are used to drive cattle through to prevent sickness. This is followed by a variety of harvest festivals, some at the beginning and some at the end of the harvest. These celebrations can be crop-specific, such as the *Fête du Biou* in Arbois in France, during which a giant grape assembled from the first harvest is brought to a church as an offering to ensure the quality of the rest of the harvest. They can also be more general, like the *Erntedankfest* celebrated in Germany and Austria, during which God is thanked for the year's harvest at the end of the season.

The rituals that emerged around these events became tools for society to make sense of the cycles of the year and to structure the year. Byung-Chul Han writes about rituals stabilizing life and, through their repetitiveness, making it last. In *The Disappearance of Rituals. A Topology of the Present*, he recognizes rituals as something that brings people together and creates an alliance, a wholeness, a community – something that is gradually disappearing as a medium for community maintenance.[2] Indeed, what seems to unite different types of celebrations is the fact that a shared moment is created around an event.

If we draw into this discourse also festivities that relate to a person's life and announce new phases of it, we recognize more clearly their different functions and how they create a shared moment: next to celebrations (birth, soil fertility), there are also rites of passage or mourning (for a person, or nature going into a non-productive mode in winter). This makes rituals appear as coping mechanisms that gather different groups of people to deal with different types of life events or natural events. These festivities and rites built a body of beliefs that would define communities that share them. When adopted by Christian cosmology, the locality of these beliefs was in part lost, detaching communities from the seasonal cycles.

Another layer of such detachment can be observed in totalitarian regimes, where seasonal celebra-

2   Byung-Chul Han, *The Disappearance of Rituals. A Topology of the Present* (Cambridge: Polity Press, 2020), 3 and 6.

Illustration of Ice Saints,
The Netherlands

Effigy of Morana representing Death, Czech Republic

Post-Seasonal Rituals

Sanctuary decorated for *Erntedankfest* (harvest festival) in a village church in Marbach, Germany

Harvest dance in Schneverdingen, Germany

Rituals

Poster for the day of harvest and collectivization, Soviet Russia

Grape procession during *La fête du Biou* in Arbois, France

Post-Seasonal Rituals

Burning of the *Maslenitsa* (Butter Week) effigy, Russia

Antique postcard with depiction of *Les Brandons* in Auvergne, France

tions were instrumentalized to strengthen ideologies. During the Nazi regime, for instance, the *Erntedankfest* formerly celebrated in communities became a nationwide festivity. At its peak, it is believed to have gathered more than a million people in one location, not only to give thanks to the farmers but mainly to increase the *Führer's* contact with the masses and to demonstrate the *Reich's* military prowess.[3] In the Soviet Union, rituals were seen as a tool to structure and maintain power relations in society, a tool for 'cultural management'.[4] Harvest Day, an ancient Russian holiday, became the 'Day of Collectivization and Harvest'. It took on "...the character of a wide political campaign, the basic content of which was the mobilization of the broad labouring masses of town and country for the cause of the socialist reconstruction of the Soviet village".[5] Although the intention behind reintroducing this holiday was, among others, the replacement of religious holidays, some new festivities *not* rooted in natural or religious timelines were established. One example is the Holiday of Hammer and Sickle, which was "designed to express the unity of interest between workers and collective farmers, between town and country".[6] What is interesting is how the term design is used

3   Gesine Gerhard, *Nazi Hunger Politics: A History of Food in the Third Reich* (Plymouth: Rowman & Littlefield, 2015), 41–43.
4   Christel Lane, *The Rites of Rulers: Ritual in Industrial Society: The Soviet Case* (New York: Cambridge University Press, 1981), 1.
5   V. N. Stolnaya, ed., *Massovye prazdniki i zrelishcha* (Moscow: Iskusstvo, 1961), 257.
6   Lane, *The Rites of Rulers*, 127.

to define the construction of a new festivity – and that it includes a new shape of festive props and attributes. In Soviet Russia, for instance, the loaf of bread traditionally baked with the newly harvested flour would be attributed with a figure symbolizing the amount of grain delivered by the farm to the state,[7] while in Soviet Ukraine the shape of a traditional corn wreath would change into a five-cornered star or be decorated with the emblems of Soviet power.[8]

The idea of intervening in seasonal rituals is therefore not new. However, the above examples indicate adaptations in festivities that remove the rituals from the natural cycles and their localities and often erase the connection to specific communities. During a discussion in the framework of *Areaal I: Rural Ritual Reality* organized by Plan B in relation to the exhibition of Seasonal Neighbours at Z33, the idea of change or transition through rituals came up; rituals were identified as a tool for provoking change.[9] A question can be posed as to whether reintroducing rituals into the new rural reality can be a tool for redefining it and reconnecting to localities in which our food production is rooted. While Byung-Chul Han isn't animated by the idea of returning to rituals due to the dangers of nostalgia that he recognizes, we have to understand

7   A. Filatov, *O novykh i starykh obryadakh* (Moscow: Profizdat, 1967), 88.

8   Lane, *The Rites of Rulers*, 124.

9   "Notes from Areaal I: Rural Ritual Reality," Kunstenplatform Plan B, March 19, 2022, https://www.kunstenplatformplanb.be/nieuws/notes-from-areaal-i-rural-ritual-reality.

that the nostalgic image of the rural reality is long gone. Therefore, it's not so much about returning to the past, but rather about reinventing the rituals according to today's agricultural realities and newly emerged narratives around it, or perhaps even reinventing the rural reality through the introduction of these rituals. From my position as a social designer, I became interested in what this could mean for navigating the post-seasonal seasonality, at the same time being conscious about the different nature of modern agriculture and ritualistic practices. Could new ritual practices counterbalance greenhouse horticulture and draw us back closer to the earth?

POST-SEASONAL ALMANAC

The rhythm of the agricultural year was traditionally documented and forecast in a farmers' almanac. Such an almanac would be a blueprint to orient oneself in time, offering information on low and high tides, moon phases, cyclical weather patterns, and sowing and harvesting times. Today, farmers' almanacs still mention weather patterns but are pretty much detached from the reality of the modern agricultural context. When describing the year, the *Enkhuizer Almanak* lists moon phases and zodiac signs next to the birthdays of the royal family and religious celebrations. In the 409th edition from the year 2004, the tradition of Easter Fires is described in connection to land fertility, which is

24

Feasting on the back of the robot

ASPARAGUS LIBERATION

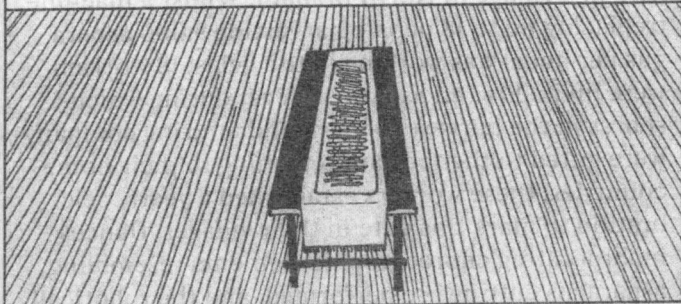

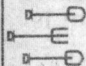

LABOUR SEASON

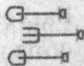

just one example of a religious celebration originating in an agricultural tradition.

My own project, the *Post-Seasonal Almanac* is an attempt to redraw the farmers' almanac according to the contemporary post-seasonal world, where the growing, harvesting, and consuming of food no longer depends on natural factors. The new notion of the almanac looks at agricultural practices and their interdependence with phenomena such as the trans-European movement of workers and goods, international politics, labour rights, and energy supply. Several events representing crucial aspects of modern agriculture are highlighted on the timeline of the year. Could such phenomena become the subject of new celebrations and rituals that introduce the invisible realities behind our food system?

Within Seasonal Neighbours, the topic of seasonal celebrations surfaced on different levels: while some trajectories approached individual themes through the lens of rituals, the *Post-Seasonal Almanac* attempted to construct a vision of the post-seasonal reality. All three projects that touched upon the theme of rituals were incorporated in the almanac, including projects by Karolina Michalik, Collectif dallas and Anastasia Eggers. They will be discussed in more detail below.

OLYMPIC FIRE OF
THE AUBERGINE SEASON

A narrative that I came across during my field-work in an aubergine greenhouse in Westland was connected to the change of season between the Netherlands and Spain, the two biggest aubergine exporters in the EU. Greenhouses in Westland have the capacity to grow aubergines all year round. However, the growing number of Spanish aubergines on the market leads to falling prices and makes the Dutch ones no longer profitable. Perhaps this relation – which is hardly visible to the consumer and yet is the driver of the aubergine season today – could be highlighted by constructing a seasonal celebration around it. With *Aubergine Season Relay*, I suggest introducing an 'Olympic Fire' of the aubergine season that would be passed on from a greenhouse in Westland in the Netherlands to a greenhouse in Almería in Spain, by using the logistics chain that normally makes the change of seasons possible.

In the first iteration of this ritual, I focused on connecting the two greenhouses by sending an object from one to the other while making the change of season visible to the logistics workers. The second iteration took place in a greenhouse in Westland and was an attempt to develop props for decorating the last truck of the aubergine season to create visibility outside. During the intervention, I invited a group of visitors to the green-

44

WEEK

A celebration of trans-European logistics

AUBERGINE SEASON RELAY

NL ES

GEOPOLITICAL SEASON

house to gather the aubergine plants about to be taken down at the end of the season and weave decorative elements that were then mounted on the truck as a test, hinting at the possibility of making the change of season visible on motorways. I thought of this ritual not only as a means to draw attention to the economically controlled season but also as a comment on the availability of local produce that is often misleading due to year-round access.

RITUALIZING INFRASTRUCTURES OF CARE

Together with the new seasonality, a new materiality of the season is arising. While the Ice Saints protected the crops by delaying the sowing times, human-made technologies or 'structures of care' that Camille Gaillard & Salomon Tyler from Collectif dallas are looking into allow the fruit orchards to flourish despite being planted before the spring frost.

In Alpine regions, the Night of Cold Sophie – Saint Sophie being the patroness of the plants against the night frost, one of the Ice Saints – is marked by lighting fires in the fields. In their research on these different typologies, Collectif dallas were fascinated by the often DIY systems they came across, together with a variety of technologized anti-frost systems such as wind tunnels, fans, sprinkling systems and fog dragons that all share the same function as Cold Sophie: protecting the fruit tree blossoms from the spring frost.

For an artistic intervention that took place during the exhibition at Z33, they designed a reinterpreted version of the traditional fire pot. Thinking about how its short and punctual use of protecting the blossoms once a year could be expanded into new social and ritualistic functions, they organized a *Sacred Fire Pot* procession. During the intervention, the act of carrying of the fire pot into the field gathered some of the actors from the orchard around their *Sacred Fire Pot*.

'POLSKOŚĆ' (POLISHNESS) IN THE EUROPEAN COUNTRYSIDE

Chłopi by Karolina Michalik directly relates to a traditional harvest celebration and its missing relation to contemporary agricultural realities. *Dożynki*, a harvest festival in Poland that was celebrated as early as the sixteenth century, was originally a folkloric event marking the end of the harvest season. A prop that stands at the heart of this festivity is the *wieniec*, a crown woven from the local grain harvest. Most indicative is the *Most Beautiful Wieniec Dozynkowy*, a national competition that every region of Poland can enter with a *wieniec* representing that region. The competition is hosted at the annual Presidential *Dozynki* and broadcast on the national television. While the celebration itself is something that emerged

13
WEEK

A welcoming ritual for the returning migrant workers

BREAD AND SALT PROCESSION

LABOUR SEASON

in pre-Christian times and the crown's materiality and aesthetics have hardly changed as it made its way into modern times, the agricultural narrative in Poland has evolved towards more complexity.

Karolina Michalik's project proposed to enter this competition, but with a *wieniec* representing the Polish seasonal workers in Belgium, stressing the importance of the Polish seasonal migratory labour within the complexities of the European agricultural system – a narrative that remains completely excluded from traditional harvest celebrations.

The seeds of this project not only lay in her fieldwork experience but also relate to Karolina's personal migration story. Having spent most of her youth in the US, she returned to Poland, her motherland, as a student at the age of 18. There, she witnessed a country that was rapidly changing because of the money and cultural exchange imported by the many Poles who had migrated for work. Paradoxically, in popular narratives, she encountered a traditional nationalistic idea of 'Polishness' and a failure to recognize the internationality of Polish people, as she considers herself to be. In her practice, Karolina therefore aims to broaden the public representation of Poland's modern rural identity, challenging the role of folklore as a tool of representation along with political agency. In her *wieniec* project, she calls into question the flexibility and adaptability of events that have been taking shape in almost the same way for centuries. At the same time, her practice investigates the power of folkloric representational tools to bring together new groups of people who might not have developed a strong sense of community yet.

RITUALIZING THE NEW RURAL

At the core of the collective's engagements with ritual was the recognition of their power and their potential to impact different groups within the agricultural context and focus on their interconnectedness. What linked the different projects was how they adapted the concepts of celebrations to the modern context. By including new and underrepresented groups in a traditional celebration, by re-pivoting the aspect of care in farming while ritualizing its new materiality, or by applying the logic of traditional celebrations to new seasonal narratives that emerged from industrial agriculture.

While *Chłopi* focuses on the topic of the presence (and absence) of European seasonal migrant workers in the Polish contemporary rural discourse, the *Sacred Firepot Procession* also involves the aspect of the workers' presence in the project's trajectory. Both interventions were planned to engage with communities: *Chłopi* required more active community participation while Collectif dallas suggested the view of seasonal workers as recipients (and therefore the audience) of care through their ritual object. *Aubergine Season Relay*, on the other hand, aimed at creating a new representation: involving mostly people already associated with the context, it observed and highlighted a hidden narrative from the post-seasonal world, bringing more understanding about the local availability of crops. As a newly invented ritual, it didn't have to fit into any pre-established framework which allows it to spread over several years with different types of ritualistic interventions that at some point will come together in the form of an established ritual. However, Karolina Michalik was faced with some challenges that gave a different form to the ritual than what she initially imagined to be doing. She was not only attempting to intervene in a large-scale festivity with a long tradition but also bridging two entities at different ends of Europe: the community of Polish workers in Belgium that yet had to be defined and the festivity in Poland. Therefore, the intervention took place on a scale of the context in which she was working in Belgium, bringing workers together around a strawberry *wieniec*.

The *Sacred Fire Pot* of Collectif dallas aimed to thematize the development of technological anti-frost solutions. As such, it indirectly touched on the topic of mediation of an existing seasonal festivity with the same function. Seeing how a saint was believed to play a role in the concept of crop protection (and other saint days were used for orientation, e.g. in sowing and harvesting times for farmers), it becomes evident that for a long time, the church played an important role as a mediator between nature and culture. Here, an artist collective attempts to reframe this moment from which the ritualistic character has been removed by technology, introducing new relationships that include seasonal workers in new infrastructures of care. With a less obvious interrelation to the Church, the other two interventions are also trying out the role of mediators: by connecting two competitors and making this link visible, or by reconnecting the identity of migrant labourers to their own country.

Because of their popular and multi-layered nature, rural rituals have enormous potential to make the invisible visible. The artistic research of Seasonal Neighbours cast a critical eye on existing rituals in relation to the reality we encountered in our fieldwork, attempting to understand the potential of redesigning these rituals. Prototyping rituals can produce critical perspectives and give new future narratives material presence.

The rituals prototyped within the collective aim to restore public awareness of the years' seasonal cycle in a different way – even if seasons no longer depend on the natural cycle of the sun. By producing objects, intervening in activities, and inviting specific people to participate we attempted to make present and tangible new and underexposed relationships between actors and contexts.

EIGHT DAYS IN WORB
BY INES

solidarity farming initiative

the hottest days of this summer
we squat, kneel, stand or bend over
we plant sugarloaf and fennel seedlings
we pick yellow beans, leek, lettuce,
 potatoes, courgettes, pumpkins, tomatoes
 and we cut basil

10 ha of arable and pasture land and 3 ha of forest

the lentil harvest has failed

next to the farm, an automatic land mower

the 'gjät' (weed) smells good and is slightly damp

sunstroke

2 farmers
2 gardeners
3 volunteers
1 employee
2 children
400 people who support the farm in some way
 or another
12 years of existence

soil under my fingernails

CHŁOPI

Tracing the Wieniec

Karolina Michalik

Sołectwo
Wola Wielka

Gmina Żyrakó

212 Chłopi

Rituals

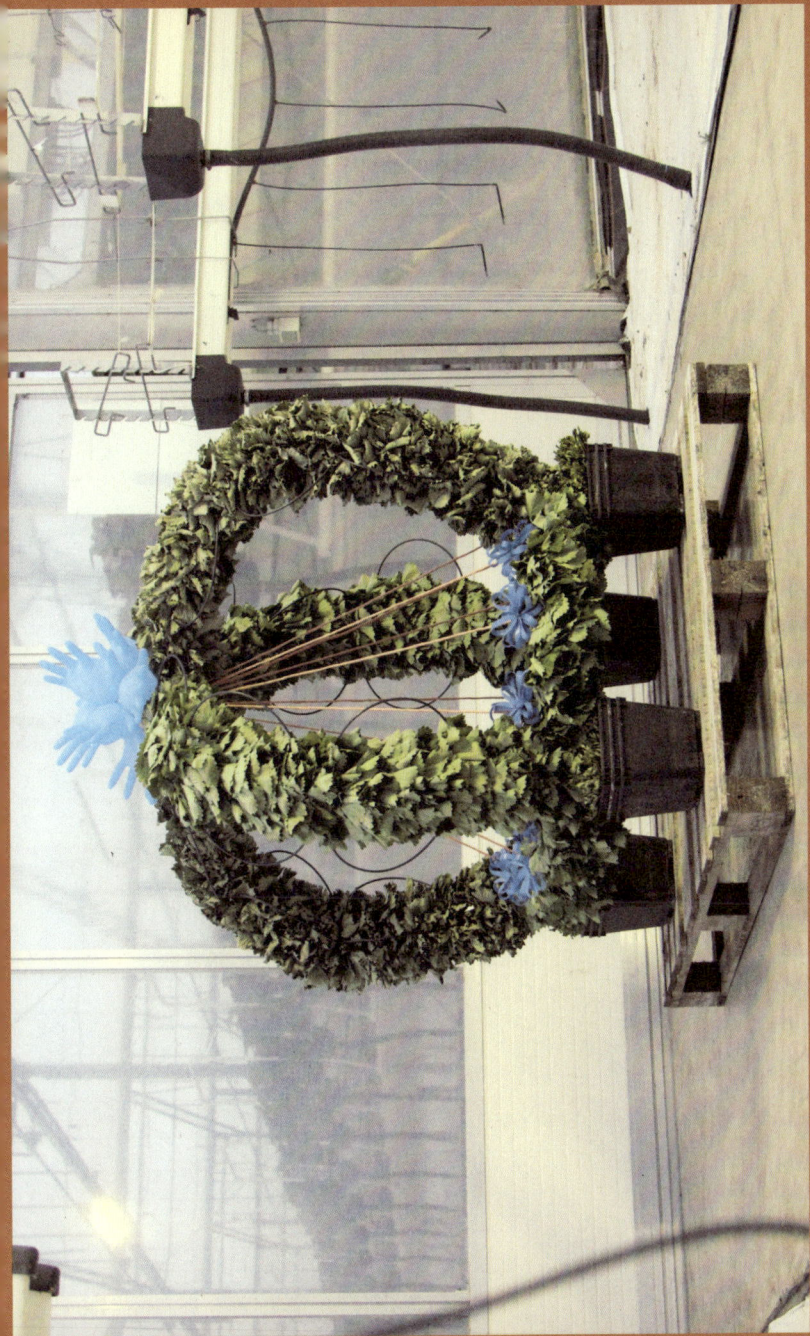

While investigating representations of *Polskość* (Polishness) through the lens of migratory seasonal labour in the Belgian countryside, Karolina Michalik looked at contemporary forms of harvest celebrations and how they act as multilayered public representations of Poland's modern rural identity.

She observed folklore being used as a colourful tool of political agency, enabling and maintaining a selective interpretation of the past and present based on nostalgic, religious and land-rooted patriotism. Trying to entangle the different cultural codes and narrative levels that enter into play, she embarked on her own journey of learning to weave a *wieniec*, a wreath or crown made from local grain harvests. During her field research, she also documented the appearance of harvest wreaths at different regional harvest celebrations around Poland, from which phenomena such as seasonal migratory work are excluded.

SEEDS AT THE TABLE

Recipes for Transnational Relations

Yacinth Pos

PULL THE EDGES IN, FOLD NEATLY
Spiced rice in mallow leaves

1	big onion
4	cloves of garlic
1	piece of ginger, the size of a thumb
6	carrots (+/-)
2 tsp	ground paprika powder
2 tsp	ground ginger powder
2 tsp	ground coriander powder
2 tsp	ground turmeric powder
2 tsp	ground cardamom powder
4 tsp	tomato paste
200 g	rice
25	mallow leaves (and flowers)
100 g	almonds
	honey
	salt

Step 1: Preparing the rice mixture
This recipe takes time, diligence and
meticulousness. Begin by finely chopping
onions and grating some garlic and ginger,
then gently fry them in a deep pan. Add
diced carrots to the aromatic mixture,
allowing their natural sweetness to enhance
the flavours. Now add the following spices:
ground paprika, ginger, coriander, turmeric
and cardamom. Incorporate a touch of
tomato paste and a dash of salt, harmoniz-
ing the flavours. While the spices and vegetables meld, cook a batch of rice. Once the

rice is cooked to perfection, let it cool and afterwards combine it with the spiced carrot mixture, gently stirring until every grain is coated. For a textural contrast, add chopped almonds or any desired nut variant. Adjust the seasoning to taste, considering a touch of honey for subtle sweetness or additional salt if needed.

Step 2: Tendering mallow leaves
Before rolling, trim the stems off the mallow leaves. Carefully rinse the leaves, cleansing them of any impurities. Steam the leaves briefly, allowing them to retain their vibrant colour and tender texture.

Step 3: Rolling and folding
With precision, roll and fold the spiced rice mixture into each individual mallow leaf. Take care to create neat and well-formed bundles that encapsulate the rice filling within the soft mallow leaves.

Step 4: Plating and presentation
Arrange the rice-stuffed mallow leaves on a plate. Enhance the presentation by garnishing with a sprinkle of golden turmeric powder and some mallow flowers.

DEEP GREEN AND A SLIGHT TANG
Nettle beer

12 l	water
5	buckets of nettle tops
1.5 kg	cane sugar
	a touch of ginger powder
2	lemons
6	tea bags (preferably black tea)
4	big pieces of fresh ginger
500 g	dried raisins
500 g	dried apricots
50 g	tartaric acid (or citric acid)
15 g	yeast
	a sealed pot or fermentation vessel

Step 1: Nettle gathering
To create a generous batch of 12 l of nettle
beer, embark on a nettle-picking adventure,
gathering about five buckets of nettle
tops measuring up to 30 cm in length from
the tip. Be cautious and use gloves during
both the picking and washing.

Step 2: Boiling the nettle leaves
Begin the beer-making process by gently
boiling the nettle leaves in approximately
12 l of water for a duration of 20 min.

Step 3: Enchanting flavours
Once the infusion is complete, incorporate
the cane sugar and stir until it dissolves

completely. Enhance the brew with the ginger powder, the essence of 2 sliced lemons, some black tea, a hint of fresh ginger, and the distinctive flavours of dried raisins and apricots. This adds an extra layer of taste to the beer.

Step 4: Fermentation process
After the composition has cooled down, introduce the tartaric acid (citric acid is also suitable) and yeast, ensuring the harmonious fermentation of the mixture. Pour this blend into a fermentation vessel or any large sealed pot, allowing it to rest undisturbed. Find a warm, shaded spot for the infusion to mature for approximately 24 hrs. Subsequently, move the vessel to a cooler location, permitting the beer to ferment for four days. Ensure the container remains securely covered throughout the process. Regularly skim off any foam that forms on the surface using a spoon while gently stirring the mixture.

Step 5: Straining and storage
To achieve optimal clarity, strain the brew before transferring it into a tightly sealed barrel. Alternatively, you can bottle the nettle beer for future enjoyment. When stored in a dark, cool place, the beer will retain its quality for about one month.

Seeds at the Table

Rituals

DRESSED IN TINTS OF RED, ORANGE AND GREEN
Minty sorrel soup

4	white onions
+/- 600 g	sorrel leaves
1 l	vegetable stock (preferably homemade)
	a chunk of butter
4 tsp	flour
	a bunch of mint
200 ml	cream
	optional: edible flowers, quail eggs, herb oil, bread

Step 1: Creating the base
Begin by cutting white onions into pieces. Gently fry half of the onions in a deep soup pot until they turn translucent. Thoroughly wash the sorrel leaves and chop them finely. Add the leaves to the pot and pour in vegetable stock on top until the sorrel is just covered.

Step 2: Simmering
Let the sorrel and onions simmer for about half an hour, allowing their flavours to meld and intensify. Once tender, transform the mixture into a puree using a hand blender, ensuring a smooth and velvety consistency.

Step 3: Enhancing the mixture
In another deep pan, gently heat some butter. Add the rest of the chopped onion to the pan, cooking it until it reaches a translucent state. Add some flour to the pan, creating a roux. Let it fry for a few minutes. Gradually pour in the sorrel puree and allow the mixture to simmer for an additional 10 min. The soup will slowly start to thicken.

Step 4: Adding some creaminess and mint
Add a big bunch of freshly cut mint and the cream. Before serving, decorate the soup with, for example, some edible flowers, quail eggs and a splash of herb oil or serve the soup with some freshly baked bread.

HIDDEN IN PLAIN SIGHT
Krokiety with a bed of chickweed

2	handfuls of chickweed
4	white onions
600 g	mushrooms
	some vegetable oil
	a pinch of sugar
6	eggs
500ml	milk
250 g	flour
	a chunk of butter
75 g	raisins
75 g	cranberries
150 g	dates
150 g	white (Polish) cheese
125 g	sour cream
400 g	bread crumbs or panko
	salt

Step 1: Preparing the chickweed
Begin by gently removing the roots of the
chickweed, ensuring each stem is free
from soil and any unwelcome visitors. Now
steam the chickweed briefly, preserving
its vibrant colours.

Step 2: Caramelizing
Cut the onions in rings and caramelize them
by softly frying them with a touch of sugar.
Finely chop the mushrooms, then gently fry
them in oil and add a sprinkle of salt.

Step 3: Creating the pancake batter
While the mushrooms and onions sizzle,
prepare a simple pancake batter. Whisk
together two eggs, the milk, flour and
a pinch of salt, until smooth. In a buttered
pan, cook the pancakes one by one until
they turn light brown.

Step 4: Crafting the filling
Soak the raisins, dates and cranberries
in warm water and cut them in small pieces.
Blend all of them with the sautéed mushrooms and caramelized onions. Add crumbled
white Polish cheese and the sour cream,
combining them into a harmonious mixture.
Taste and add some salt if needed.

Step 5: Assembling
Generously spread the filling inside each
pancake, creating a bed of steamed chickweed on top of it. Roll like a burrito, ensuring the filling remains securely tucked
within. Beat the rest of the eggs and dip
each rolled krokiety inside, then coat them
in crispy bread crumbs or panko.

Step 6: Crispy exterior
Now heat some oil in a pan and place the
krokiety in it. Gently fry them until they
reach a crispy and golden brown state.
Serve immediately; you can cut them into
smaller pieces to share.

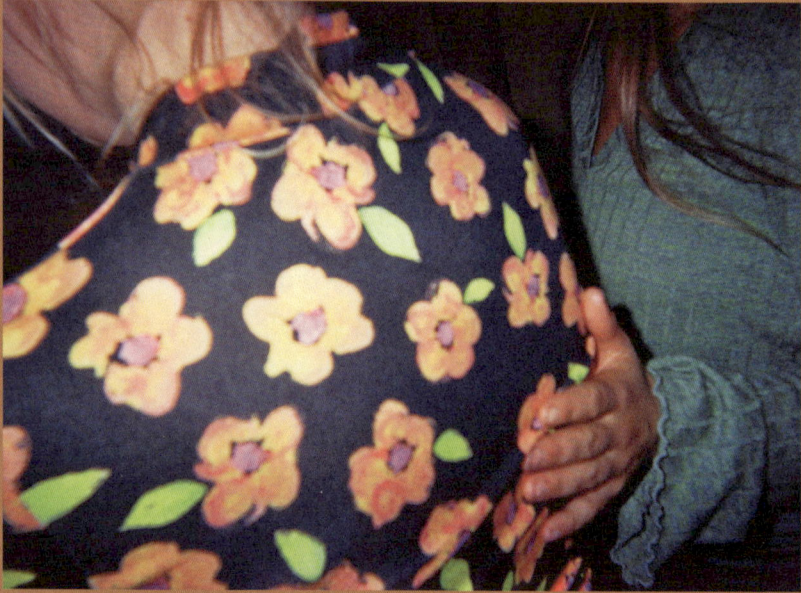

Seeds at the Table

Rituals

ACROSS LONG DISTANCES
Pierogi in nettle sauce

375 g	flour
1	beaten egg
3 tsp	vegetable oil
230 ml	cold water
4	handfuls of nettle tops
3	white onions
	a splash of white wine
500 ml	cream
	some icing sugar
+/- 6	sweet potatoes
2	bunches of chives
1	bunch of parsley
	pepper & salt
	optional garnish: beurre noisette, white cheese, fresh herbs

Step 1: Preparing the dough
Combine the flour, eggs, vegetable oil, water and a touch of salt. Now gently knead the ingredients together. Add more water if needed; the dough needs to be smooth and pliable. Allow the dough to rest for an hour.

Step 2: Handling the nettles
Clean the nettles thoroughly under cold water. Blanch the nettles in salted water for a few minutes, rinse with cold water afterwards.

Step 3: Crafting the nettle sauce
Prepare the sauce by cutting the onions
roughly and softly frying them in a saucepan
until they turn translucent. Deglaze the onions with white wine, adding cream and the
blanched nettles. Simmer the sauce to reduce
it slightly and use a hand blender until the
sauce achieves a smooth consistency. Add a
pinch of salt, pepper and a hint of sugar.

Step 4: Filling the dumplings
For the filling, peel and cut sweet potatoes
into small pieces before boiling until they
become tender. Once cooked, remove from
the water and allow to cool slightly. Hand
mash the sweet potatoes and then combine
them with finely chopped chives, parsley,
salt, pepper and a hint of icing sugar.

Step 5: Rolling and assembling
Roll out the dough until it's 2 mm thick.
Use a cup to create circles for enclosing the
filling. Fold the circles in half, creating
half-moon shapes.

Step 6: Serving the delightful pierogi
Once the pierogi have been boiled to perfection, serve them immediately, generously
smothering them in the green nettle sauce.
Garnish with, for example, a delicious
beurre noisette, a crumbled white cheese
and some fresh cut herbs.

This collection of recipes sprouted from a strong desire to dive deeper into the world of seasonal work. Over time, Yacinth Pos crossed paths with many individuals who travelled to the Netherlands for temporary employment, using food as a medium to gather and exchange. Her curiosity about recipes from their home countries and the use of local flora served as a way to connect. These personal encounters formed the basis of this series of recipes and eventually ended up on a communal table, where those she had met during this experience were warmly welcomed.

UNPACKING ROUTINES OF ARRIVAL

Arrivals, Routines and Rituals of Migration and Agriculture in Westland and Haspengouw

Carolien Lubberhuizen

Carolien Lubberhuizen is an anthropologist and PhD candidate at Utrecht University and KU Leuven. Her research is part of the Horizon2020 project ReROOT. It explores arrival infrastructures surrounding agricultural labour migration in Westland and Haspengouw. She uses ethnographic, participatory and creative research methods to understand how these arrival infrastructures interact with and (re)produce precarity, (im)mobility, temporality and orientations towards the future. In this article she reflects on the pop-up exhibition she co-curated with Winona Boomkens, as part of her creative and participatory methods of research.

The small Church of Guvelingen in Sint-Truiden is packed with people: neighbours, visitors from other areas of the country, a choir, local politicians, children and even a special ceremonial 'fruit committee'.[1] They have all gathered on a rainy Sunday in late April to celebrate and 'bless' the fruit trees in blossom. Though this fruit-related ceremony or agricultural ritual was only brought into existence in the 1950s, the 2023 edition features a full programme that includes a procession that makes its way to the school of agriculture and a ceremonial blessing of the blossom as well as of bees, pets, cyclists and tractors. As one of the most important events of the tourist season in Sint-Truiden, it plays a crucial role in promoting and reproducing the

1   The 'Keizerlijke Commanderie' (Imperial Commandry) is a regional organization whose activities include promoting and acting as ambassadors for local fruit production. They organize events, ceremonies and competitions.

local agricultural heritage of the fruit-producing region of Haspengouw. During the ceremony, the 'local' nature of fruit production in Haspengouw is celebrated, and fruit farmers are thanked for their labour (and all the hardship that comes with it) and for providing us with food.

Agriculture involves a great deal of hard work and a lot of uncertainty due to unpredictable weather conditions and a changeable market. As any anthropological account of agricultural communities will show, the celebration of rituals around important seasonal moments is a way to deal with this uncertainty, whether for sowing, during the blossoming or after a period of hard work during the harvest period. They also serve a social purpose, bringing people together to share stories, experiences and knowledge across different social groups and generations. However, it is remarkable that these rituals mostly reinforce certain narratives of agricultural heritage while excluding others. Rituals such as the blessing of the fruit trees in blossom mainly emphasize the 'local' and the 'traditional', despite the drastic changes in agriculture over the past century that have connected rural regions with international locations and people through the intensification of agriculture, labour and technological innovation.

After more than a year of ethnographic research on agricultural labour migration in Westland and Haspengouw, the total absence and invisibility of the people actually working in the fields in these contemporary types of rituals and celebrations of agricultural heritage was striking. On the one hand, this absence seemed to contradict the intimate, albeit complicated and tense connections that have developed between workers, farmers and plants. On the other hand, their absence also reflects the invisibility of migrant workers, and more importantly the lack of accessible information, rights and other support resources offered by governments or other local institutions. In fact, both these connections in the fields and greenhouses *and* disconnections in more formal structures shape the way migrant workers navigate these places and contexts of agriculture, labour and migration.

Together with migrant workers in Haspengouw and Westland and with the help of farmers and peasant organizations in Romania and Moldova, the research resulted in the exhibition *Picking Fruit, Sowing Stories*. It explores how rituals like the blessing of the blossoming trees could be a space to renegotiate this interplay of connection and disconnection. With the notion of arrival infrastructures[2] and guided by new, intimate and everyday routines of different people and processes 'arriving' in Westland and Haspengouw, this essay reflects on translocal connections of agricul-

---

2   Bruno Meeus, Bas van Heur and Karel Arnaut, "Migration and the Infrastructural Politics of Urban Arrival." *Arrival Infrastructures: Migration and Urban Social Mobilities*, ed. Bruno Meeus, Karel Arnaut and Bas van Heur, (Cham: Palgrave Macmillan, 2019), 1-32.

tural labour migration in Europe's rural and urban areas. I argue that reworking these routines of arrival into new rituals and intervening these into existing ones, could be a productive way to, in the words of Nirmal Puwars, 'reroute accounts and visceral experiences'[3] of agriculture and (seasonal) migration. Before diving into these infrastructures and routines, it is necessary to briefly contextualize the two 'fields' of my fieldwork.

THE FIELDS: WESTLAND AND HASPENGOUW

Westland and Haspengouw are as alike as they are different. Firstly, Westland is an administrative municipality to the west of The Hague and Rotterdam, comprising several towns, whereas Haspengouw is a cultural and geophysical region in the Belgian province of Limburg comprising several municipalities. Both are, however, historically and internationally known for their horticultural industries: fruit horticulture and greenhouse agriculture, respectively. Secondly, agriculture and migration[4] in both Westland and Haspengouw have a historical relation through labour that precedes the enlargement of the European Union. When growers in the 1980s and 1990s could not meet labour demands, Turkish and Moroccan guest workers were em-

---

3 Nirmal Puwar, "Noise of the Past: Spatial Interruptions of War, Nation, and Memory," *The Senses and Society 6*, no. 3 (2011): 326.
4 Throughout this essay, the terms 'migration' and 'migrant workers' are used to emphasize that these labour trajectories not only include seasonal, cyclical or temporary ones, but are more diverse than implied by categories such as seasonal worker.

ployed. In Haspengouw, undocumented Sikh refugees from the Punjab found informal employment as fruit pickers. Together with national legislations that allow for more flexible and temporary labour, the enlargement of the EU in 2004 and 2007 provided new possibilities for both farmers looking for extra 'hands' and new EU citizens looking for work and financial opportunities. From these emerging mobilities, (in)formal transnational migration industries developed in which employment agencies, farmers and brokers became important, benefiting actors in channelling agricultural migrant workers into temporary work and housing. Whereas in Haspengouw this mostly entails informal recruitment, a seasonal and non-contractual work status and remote housing on or near the orchards, growers in Westland outsource labour to employment agencies that offer temporary, zero-hour contracts and housing facilities of varying quality. Even though in both countries national attempts have been made to counteract exploitation, local municipalities and residents in Westland and Haspengouw regard migrant workers as economically important but not necessarily as co-citizens occupying a structural place in the region.

ARRIVAL INFRASTRUCTURES

From these historical, commercial and local developments in Haspengouw and Westland, so-called migration infrastructures have emerged. With this notion, migration researchers Xiang and Lindquist have tried to understand how (labour) migration is mediated by both state and non-state actors.[5] In Westland and Haspengouw, these infrastructural interlinkages are explicitly present and powerful in the form of commercial actors, brokers and EU labour regimes that mediate labour mobility. My own research looked specifically at arrival infrastructures, a framework proposed by Bruno Meeus[6] and his colleagues to understand the places, technologies, practices, institutions, networks and services that newcomers become entangled in during their arrival, mediating their futures as well as their aspirations. Looking from the point of view of arrival structures allows for a more relational perspective. This also means seeing different agricultural and urban areas not as separate spaces, but as connected and shaping each other through the translocal infrastructuring acts of people, mobilities, objects, stories, remittances and more. The following examples encountered during fieldwork will help us to understand these arrival infrastructures more concretely.

5   Biao Xiang and Johan Lindquist, "Migration Infrastructure," *American Behavioral Scientist 48*, issue 1 (2014)
6   Meeus, van Heur and Arnaut, *Migration and the Infrastructural Politics of Urban Arrival*, 1–32.

The first example starts in a Polish shop in Schiedam near Rotterdam, where many migrant workers employed in Westland are housed. At the counter, there was a display of various flyers. One of them had been distributed by an NGO for Polish women and apparently had travelled from the Polish shops in The Hague to this small supermarket in Schiedam. The flyer promoted one of the many information sessions the NGO organizes about labour unions, sick leave and unemployment insurance. At the next information session, Polish newcomers travelled from Westland, Schiedam, Vlaardingen and other towns of the region to the small community centre in The Hague. Urban infrastructures, objects, social networks and informal infrastructuring practices came together in these Polish shops, which usually cater not only to Polish newcomers but also to people looking for Bulgarian, Romanian or Baltic products. These kinds of shops therefore function not only as places where familiar products can be found, but also as places where migrant workers can access relevant information, services and resources provided by NGOs, municipalities and commercial actors that can help them to manage their arrival.

The second example centres around Pjotr, a Polish man who started working on an orchard in Zepperen, Haspengouw, ten years ago. He now works all year round, with a permanent contract. He is also responsible for gathering a group of around fifty friends and (extended) family members from a small town in the province of Świętokrzyskie to come and work on the orchard in Zepperen. When the farmers need more people than he can find through his personal connections, Pjotr uses a local Facebook page to promote the message. He also helps to arrange a large bus travelling to and from Poland, delivers all the administrative information necessary to employ the new workers, and explains daily to the workers what needs to be done. Being trusted by both workers and farmers, he has become a central actor in connecting the population of this rural town in Poland to the orchard in another rural town in Haspengouw. Consequently, he has become a crucial part of the arrival infrastructure, as he has not only knowledge and experience of the orchard, but also the contacts and social networks to help new seasonal workers in their (re)arrival process.

ROUTINES OF ARRIVAL

Our research on arrival infrastructures resulted in an exhibition aimed at opening up to creative and participatory intervention. *Picking Fruit, Sowing Stories* opened during the blessing ceremony in Sint-Truiden. It featured photos of daily routines and rituals made by migrant workers as well as ethnographic and interactive objects from the orchards. These pictures and objects were accompanied by an audioscape, created in collaboration with human geographer Noor van der Vorst. The audioscape, called *New Sounds and Rhythms of*

Fruit Horticulture[7], is a compilation of recordings of everyday sounds from contemporary horticulture: the repetitive sounds of picking strawberries, the daily commute with other pickers, the cacophony of different languages spoken at the same time, the Polish rap songs in the kitchen of the housing facilities. Placing this immersive scene in the unusual setting of the church during the ceremony, the exhibition confronted the audience with the unseen mechanisms, regimes and (non)human relations at work. Some of these photos and objects will now be introduced to unpack four 'routines' of arrival.

ROUTINE OF ARRIVAL #1:
THE PLUKKAART AND ARRIVAL THROUGH REGISTRATION

Farmers all agree that administration has become an increasingly important part of their daily work. A large part of this administration concerns the registration of seasonal or migrant workers. In fact, this is one of the first things that needs to be arranged when a worker arrives. In Haspengouw, one document in particular has taken on almost totemic power in recent decades. This is the *plukkaart*, or picking card, without which seasonal workers cannot work and farmers cannot employ seasonal workers. Every day, farmers are required to register all workers on the picking card and

7   The complete sound recording can be found on pickingfruitsowingstories.com.

online via the Dimona system.[8] The *plukkaart* was introduced to formalize a seasonal work status, but the number of days seasonal workers are allowed to work with this special type of document has increased from twenty-five in the 1990s to sixty-five until the pandemic, and recently to a hundred days. For farmers like Marieke[9], filling in the *plukkaart* and Dimona system every morning is a demanding task: 'The administration is difficult because you never know who will come to work and when. And there might be an inspection, so everything has to be in order.' For pickers like Manjit, this administrative routine of filling in the picking card remains mysterious: 'You don't know whether the boss has registered you for that day nor from what time, and inspection only starts from 8 o'clock, while you start at 7 o'clock.'

Filling in the *plukkaart* might be a routine practice for farmers and seasonal workers, but at the same time the (sometimes mysterious) way farmers use the *plukkaart* to exert control over labour also reveals the delicate interdependence between farmers and seasonal workers.

8   The Dimona (Déclaration Immédiate/Onmiddellijke Aangifte) is an electronic system all Belgian employers must use to register a new employee with the National Social Security Office (Rijksdienst voor Sociale Zekerheid, RSZ).

9   All quotes throughout this essay are taken from my own research interviews with farmers and migrant workers. To ensure anonymity, the names are pseudonyms.

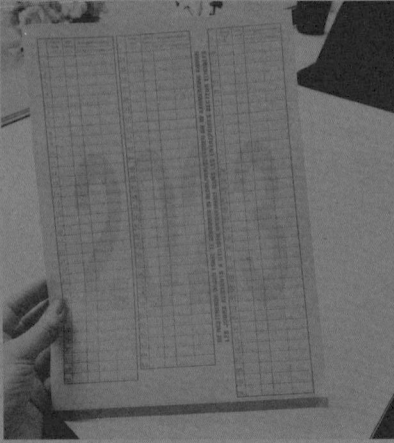

ROUTINE OF ARRIVAL #2:
ARRIVAL OF THE CHERRY SEASON

When the cherry season arrives, usually around June, cherries not only need to be picked, but also sorted. Elżbieta took this photo in the summer of 2022, her first time working in the orchard. There are piles of cherries, sorted into different categories, although for the untrained eye it is difficult to identify the markers. Sorting means getting rid of the ones without stem, categorizing and gathering cherries of the same colour, size and hardness. As the timestamp at the bottom of the picture suggests, this work is usually done each day at the end of the afternoon, after all the strawberries have been picked. Moreover, the job is done almost exclusively by the same small group of Polish women. Like the cherries, migrant workers are 'sorted' and categorized, before they even arrive, into categories of 'good' or 'bad' workers. For example, many farmers in Haspengouw prefer Polish women for picking strawberries and sorting cherries. Their hands are 'softer', they have a 'good mentality' and are willing to work hard and fast quietly. Embodied, gendered and racialized categorizations like these create labour hierarchies and shape interpersonal relations in the field. However, just as you might find a misfit cherry in your store-bought container of cherries, small acts of resistance and solidarity occur, transgressing and undoing these categorizations.

ROUTINE OF ARRIVAL #3:
ARRIVAL AT HOTEL WESTLAND

Two photos, the same radiator, the same room, different seasonal decorations. The photos were taken by two Croatian friends and roommates, Marija and Mirjana, living in a 15 m² room in Hotel Westland. For many migrant workers arriving in Westland, this hotel is one of the first spaces they encounter after their journey, and therefore an important arrival infrastructure. It is one of the few large-scale housing facilities for migrant workers in Westland, owned and managed by one of the employment agencies. The hotel, with daily inspections and 24-hour surveillance, is also emblematic of the conditions under which migrant workers are tolerated and hosted in Westland. This is the second housing facility Marija and Mirjana have been moved to since their arrival in Westland, but they have been sharing this room for more than a year now. Even though Marija and Mirjana can be moved out any moment, each season or holiday they put up new decorations to make themselves feel at home. Their routine shows how even within these temporary spaces and even when people intend to stay somewhere only temporarily, they put an effort into creating a sense of home and belonging.

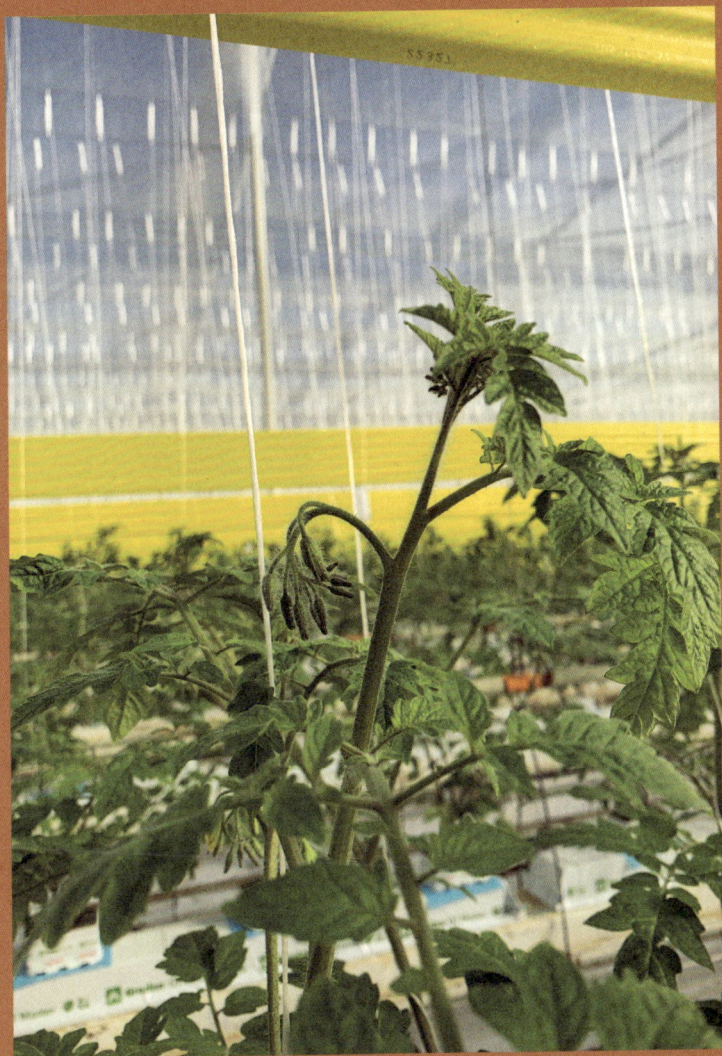

Rituals

'ROUTINE OF ARRIVAL #4:
ARRIVAL OF THE SUN

When we asked Gabriel, a specialist in tomato cultivation from Romania working in a greenhouse in Westland, to share a glimpse of his everyday work, he sent us this photo along with the following description: 'Enjoying the sun – I took this picture in an unheated greenhouse where each ray of sunlight brings happiness to both the plants and myself.'

As a result of the energy crisis, many greenhouses made the decision to reduce heating or turn off the lights. This decision had various consequences for migrant workers in an industry that is known for manipulating conditions to ensure year-round productivity. They were either given fewer working hours or were simply let go. This situation exemplifies how not only the weather and seasonal changes, like the 'arrival' of the sun in spring, but also the global economy, and geopolitical developments are interconnected with the trajectories of migrant workers. We included this photo since this simple moment of joy – shared by someone whose job is relatively secure compared to those employed through zero-hour contracts – hints at the complex layers of time that converge in agricultural labour migration. Tempos of work dictating productivity, times of family members back home, the daily insecurity of zero-hour contracts, but also long-term aspirations and dreams: many different temporalities (infra)structure the everyday lives and routines of migrant workers.

ROUTINE INTERVENTIONS

While anthropological theory generally considers rituals like the above one in Sint-Truiden as being distinct from the everyday, the mundane routines portrayed by the visual material presented in this essay and in the exhibition *Picking Fruit, Sowing Stories* deliberately attempts to blur this distinction. This approach was inspired by Nirmal Puwar and her project *Noise of the Past*, a postcolonial intervention she launched at Coventry Cathedral in 2008. In this church, which had become an important space of World War II commemoration, Puwar curated and co-created different sounds, languages and visual immersions to interrupt taken-for-granted narratives of war and death that often overlook the involvement of people from the former colonies. Similarly, our exhibition aimed to question and disrupt taken-for-granted and often romanticized narratives and rituals of rural and agricultural heritage, including the absence of migrant workers. Despite their long history of labour in the local fields, they still do not really have a place in these stories.

This interruptive intervention succeeded in part. The exhibition was granted a relatively central role in the ceremony and we got the chance to introduce and emphasize the absence of seasonal workers during the service. An agricultural heritage organization was inspired to include more stories of migration and labour. The largest challenge was, ironically, also the starting point of the exhibition: the physical absence of seasonal workers during the ceremony and exhibition. Even though audiovisual material has the potential to reverse hierarchical relations in a research project, the main people we wanted to place at the centre of our intervention were eventually only represented through their photos, voices and objects which we, as researchers, curated. The power of this act of curation would have been much stronger if it had been developed collaboratively with the migrant workers that contributed to the exhibition. Perhaps you could even say the real 'participants' in our intervention were not so much migrant workers, but the audience that visited the church: farmers, various representatives, local policymakers and other local residents.

The exhibition elicited a variety of reactions among these visitors. Some farmers reiterated defensively that working and housing conditions have improved since the early days and that they cannot run their farms otherwise. Other farmers started sharing memories of celebratory dinners with all the workers to mark the end of the harvest season. A strong common thread nevertheless ran through the diverse reactions: an acknowledgement of the invisible connections between the blessing ceremony, the seasonal workers and even the farmers and peasants in Romania and Moldova. But most importantly, for the workers able to follow their contributions either in person or through social media, the exhibition felt like an act of recognition. After seeing the exhibition, Elżbieta shared that it felt special and important to show other people 'how hard the work in the field actually is'.

Though the exhibition itself did not fully succeed in interrupting the modes of exclusion present in contemporary rural narratives, it managed to open up some of its central questions to a wider public and could be repeatedly, and routinely, put forward by everyone involved in making agriculture and migration more sustainable and fair: In what ways can we collectively celebrate, bless and remember those people whose hands too often stay invisible in our own agricultural narratives and rituals? And, whether through art, activism, politics or simple acts of hospitality, how can we reimagine and introduce more inclusive routines of accommodation, care and solidarity?

ONE MONTH IN HAASDONK
BY KAROLINA

1 greenhouse, 1 outdoor area

3 sectors inside, 3 sectors outside

planting of each sector is staggered in order to have constant rotation from March to September

all sectors in greenhouse are replanted once mid-season

you can get around 3 good harvests from each plant

'everything depends on the weather'

around 14 to 20 people working throughout the season, a few staying on longer, some briefly coming and going

'official hours' and 'unofficial hours', no difference in pay

tasks include: planting seedlings, separating flowers from rest of plant, spreading bags with insects, picking, removing plants

accommodation inside greenhouse, 2 people per room, 7 rooms, 2 toilets, 1 shower, 1 washing machine

Friday: shopping day. finish work at 17:00 to get to stores before closing

work on most Saturdays and Sundays

average day in high season:

6:00: start work

9:00: 15 min. break

12:00: 30 min. break

15:00: 15 min. break

17:00: either finish work (rarely) or 15 min. break

18:00 – 19:00 finish work

19:00 – 22:00 take your place in the shower lineup, eat dinner, prepare next day's lunch, laundry, talk, laugh, call loved ones, fall asleep

Epilogue

ATHLETES IN THE ART OF HOPING: FUTURING RELATIONS TO THE RURAL

Conversation with Sébastien Marot

Claire Chassot, Ciel Grommen and
Maximiliaan Royakkers

In 2019 the exhibition *Taking the Country's Side* was shown for the first time at the Lisbon Architecture Triennale. It explored the relationship between agriculture and architecture, two complementary practices of *domestication* which started to emerge some 10,000 years ago. The basic premise of the exhibition was that, considering the environmental challenges of today, both disciplines have to develop fundamentally in conjunction with each other. Next to a comprehensive historical overview of key works from both fields, a compass was presented with four drawings that represent different future scenarios for the interplay between our urban and rural landscape. These scenarios are the subject of our interview with Sébastien Marot, one of the main curators. We invited him to go over the scenarios with a particular focus on the people working in these environments, and the different forms of cohabitation they engage in.

Sébastien Marot is a French philosopher whose research focuses on the genealogy of contemporary theories and practices in architecture, urban planning and landscape architecture. In addition to his editorial and critical activities, Marot teaches at a number of architecture schools in Europe and the United States.

Athletes in the Art of Hoping

FOUR SCENARIOS[1]

#1

INCORPORATION: THE HIGHLY CAPITALISTIC METROPOLIS ABSORBS AGRICULTURE

What if the industrialization of agriculture and its subjection to capitalism were logically leading to its urbanization, or to its incorporation by the metropolis? Such is more or less the common accelerationist belief of those who, confronted with the dire environmental consequences of industrialized agriculture, imagine that the remedy is in the poison, and that only a flight forward into high-tech innovation and concentration may hold the key to a globally liveable future. Mega-glasshouses, vertical farms, high-rise feedlot buildings: thanks to the breakthrough and disruptive technologies of soilless culture, hydroponics and closed-system recycling, agricultural productions liberate their vast outlying peri-urban footprints.

In this perspective, much embraced by the champions of eco-modernism, eco-pragmatism and agritecture, the metropolis is clearly envisioned not just as the manifest destiny of humankind, but also as the ultimate condition of our whole biosphere. Meanwhile, the dense city acts as a control tower surveying Countryside 2.0, consisting of a

1 "Compass," Sébastien Marot, *Agriculture and Architecture: Taking the Country's Side,* https://agriculture-architecture.net/Compass.

Athletes in the Art of Hoping

grid of robotized *latifundias*,[2] interspersed with patches of productive forests, mines, natural reserves and escapist leisure resorts, all scientifically managed by an army of experts.

#2
INTEGRATION: AGRICULTURE BECOMES AN INTEGRAL COMPONENT OF URBAN EXTENSIONS

This is the latent narrative of what we might call agricultural urbanism (as a counterpoint to urban agriculture). Cities and metropolises take up spaces and species of agricultural production as integral components in the design of their margins and extensions. This perspective challenges the modern demarcation line between urban, natural and agricultural zones. Agriculture, husbandry, horticulture and forestry are hired by planning to foster an evolution of urban forms and modes of production. Park-orchards and park-nurseries, market-gardens, housing developments, open campuses which mix education, agroecology and various activities, eco- and agro-districts, greenbelts and corridors of agroforestry, etcetera: these are just some of the many new hybrid species that combine the interests of cities and agriculture. They counter the deleterious dynamics of the metabolic rift between city and

---

2   A latifundium (Latin: latus, 'spacious' and fundus, 'farm, estate') was originally the term used by ancient Romans for great landed estates specializing in agriculture destined for sale: grain, olive oil or wine. In the modern colonial period, the word was borrowed in Portuguese and Spanish for similar extensive agricultural land.

country and might also erode the persistent frontier between main job, secondary occupation and leisure activities.

Unsurprisingly, several of today's most influential approaches and trends in urban design, such as 'landscape urbanism' and 'ecological urbanism', more or less embrace this narrative of negotiation. They thus promote the idea of a 'horizontal metropolis' which, far from containing and densifying the city against a backdrop of nature and agriculture, strive on the contrary to integrate and nurture the latter within the metropolitan fabric and field.

#3
INFILTRATION: AGRICULTURE AND HORTICULTURE INVADE THE CITY

This scenario is the underlying narrative of those who take advantage of the neglected surfaces of cities and metropolises – such as roofs, terraces, vacant lots, median strips and sidewalks – to reintroduce horticulture and feeder gardening within the urban landscape; but also those in the hinterland who, reviving the practices of market gardening, build-up local networks and bypass the circuits of large-scale food business and retail. Without undermining the logic and realities of the urban condition, these varied initiatives take hold of food cultivation and consumption as a means of building up collectives and solidarity-based practices in the uprooted territories of the metropolis. Although it may be encouraged by local authorities, infiltration is essentially a bottom-up phenomenon, an opportunistic and ad-hoc logic of self-organization that does not pertain to planning. However, in contexts of severe economic decline or breakdown, such as the ones faced by Havana (and Cuba in general) during the Special Period and the City of Detroit after the collapse of its automobile industry, this phenomenon may obviously take on the dimensions of a landslide and significant recapture of urban plots by individual or collective food cultivation practices. Since economic and energy crises are likely to strike a growing number of large metropolises and urban regions in the near future, one may expect this scenario of infiltration to increasingly spread over larger metropolitan territories where it would evolve in a variety of 'rurban' fabrics, forms and syntaxes.

#4
SECESSION: 'IL FAUT CONSTRUIRE L'HACIENDA'

In this narrative of decentralization, people are dedicated to building means to achieve a significant degree of local autonomy. Urbanism is supplanted by the techniques of design and cultivation that enable people to tend a living landscape, a resilient community of interdependent humans, plants and animals. Alongside several other movements, ranging from agrarianism to libertarian

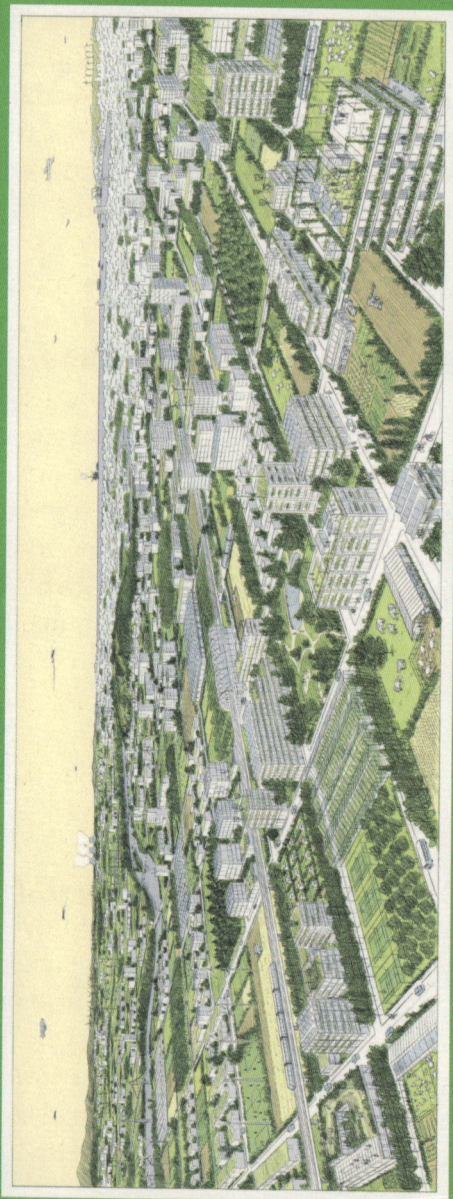

Athletes in the Art of Hoping

Epilogue

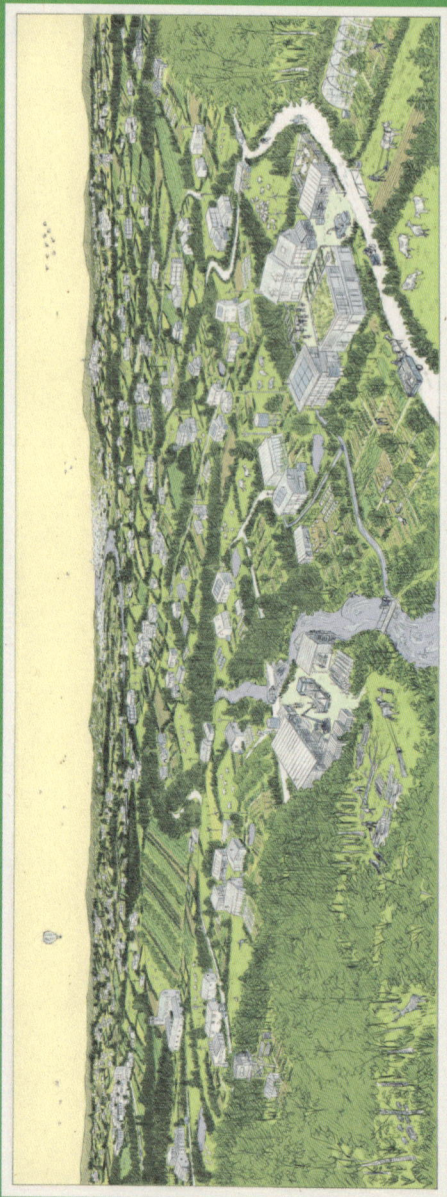

Athletes in the Art of Hoping

municipalism, permaculture is among the most disciplined expressions of this agenda.

Designating these experiments of non-urban foundation or re-foundation as 'secession' may seem excessive. Many of these experiments are not necessarily framed as the antithesis to the metropolitan ethos but sometimes as simple offshoots or havens of 'transition'. Three things must be underlined here. Firstly, these initiatives aren't convinced that the narrative of urbanization is the manifest destiny of humankind. Secondly, there is great curiosity among participants in these initiatives as to how to learn from one another, which turns them into the most active and prospective research centres. Finally, there is an intelligence and energy that participants manage to draw from the positive faith (or at least from the suspension of disbelief) that other natural covenants are eminently desirable, possibly achievable and absolutely necessary.

SN: Let's start with the first scenario, incorporation. It is an extreme future scenario we often find represented in architecture exhibitions about the countryside.[3] Farms are run by entrepreneurs, investors and engineers (agricultural as well as mechanical) and work is mostly done by robots. The narratives are often silent about the workers who, albeit in lesser numbers, work and inhabit these industrial agricultural environments. But, during our fieldwork, we have been to places that made us think a lot about this scenario. Especially in the Netherlands – Westland, and Flevoland – we worked alongside migrant labourers in large-scale aubergine greenhouses and on vast beet fields. In what kind of environment do you envision the agricultural workers to live: segregated in the countryside or integrated in the dense urban fabric?

SM: I read an article this morning about a pig factory in a Chinese metropolis. It showed two buildings, each housing 600,000 pigs. They looked like slabs from the 1960s or 1970s, huge and very deep,

3   For instance, *Countryside, The Future,* curated by AMO (Rem Koolhaas and Samir Bantal) at the Guggenheim Museum in New York, 2020–21, or the research project Automated Landscapes developed since 2017 by Het Nieuwe Instituut in Rotterdam.

with elevators on the sides. The workers of these pig factories were also living in these 'Noah's arches'. I don't know if they were migrants or from remote rural areas in China, but in any case they would only leave those urban pig factories during one six-day slot each month.

> That is incredible, but maybe not so different from the Dutch situation, where workers live in enclaves or what they call 'Polish Hotels'. These can be large, prefabricated buildings or holiday park-like sites, mostly set in the middle of nowhere, developed by investors and inhabited by two or three hundred people at a time that work on different farms and go back and forth every day. They are completely cut off from the social fabric, because of course, these 'hotels' are built on cheap land and far away to avoid any social or political tension. It's also linked to the idea of creating a market out of this. The farmer is no longer the direct employer of the seasonal workers. An intermediary agency earns a commission on the work and an investor, who collaborates with the agency, develops the buildings.

Yes, both situations are possible, either metropolitan enclaves or 'camps' in the countryside (out of sight, out of mind), or industrial factories of animal or plant biomass within cities themselves. Both are typical examples of the highly capitalistic narrative of incorporation.

> In the incorporation scenario, non-productive land or wildlife areas can be distinguished. What about wild-life in the other scenarios?

In the highly capitalist logic of the incorporation strategy, one indeed considers wildlife areas and protects them as parks, visited only by scientists, biologists, zoologists and so on. In the other scenarios, it's not so obvious. In the second scenario, wildlife exists as the border of the progression of the constant negotiation between city and countryside, and it is 'integrated' further on, in management policies that combine preservation with leisure and touristic resorts and amenities. As for the infiltration of agriculture in the metropolis, one can also imagine an infiltration of wildlife: places in a city that you leave to self-regenerate, new kinds of 'bosco-urbanity'. In the secession one, wildlife is maybe only considered as a kind of forest in the old sense of the term. In a permaculture garden there is 'the 5th zone', where nature is in automatic pilot, an area of pure observation and foraging. You can find an idea of that in the left corner of the image, but we didn't really address that.

> This could be an argument in favour
> of incorporation: industrial agriculture
> makes it possible to preserve some
> wildlife areas.

Yes, I think there is a kind of objective alliance between the incorporation scenario and the way wildlife is identified. A book that really interested me in this respect is *The Whole Earth Discipline* by Stewart Brand, published in 2009. It is a very well written argument in favour of centralization and incorporation. He writes that the environmental predicament has become so important and so urgent that it can only be dealt with in a concentrated way. Only with GMOs can we satisfy the hunger of billions of people. Cities have to become extremely dense, so you can control population growth. Energy should be nuclear. And so on. Of course, there are big issues like nuclear waste, but the argument is that these externalities are concentrated (hence manageable), not diffuse like carbon dioxide emissions. The same logic applies to wildlife: if people lived in very dense metropolises, then wildlife could, so they hope, expand on larger territories. And those territories reclaimed by 'Nature' would be segregated areas, where humans are not allowed, except for scientists and specialists: new kinds of 'parks' (excluding people) produced by a new step in the logic of capital accumulation.

> Unlike Brand, you clearly advocate the
> latter scenario, namely secession, as

the most decentralized scenario. Does
this mean you don't believe in formally
planned agriculture? Or is this just to
counterbalance the dominant narrative?

When you prepare an exhibition, you don't tend to
be subtle. Our scenarios are a kind of caricature.
I see them all developing, and I hear discourses
that fit more or less each of them. They are narratives, directions, orientations. They are not exclusive to one another: they are all happening and all
have a part of truth and consistency in them. The
secession scenario seems to be the least thought
of in the architectural sphere, while it is the one
that I find the most inspiring. It makes me happy,
or hopeful, so to speak. I also try to do as much as
I can to move in that direction myself.

But embracing this scenario doesn't mean that you
can simply discard the others. For instance, I think
that the infiltration scenario is important too, and
in fact complementary to secession. I can also understand that integration is great for architects
since it can be seen as a new (and green) narrative
or plea for building and planning. Some good work
is being attempted here and there in that direction.
As for the first scenario, even though it inspires a
basic diffidence in me, I can understand why it
may appear, in certain situations, as the only reasonable hope. If you live in Singapore or Hong
Kong, for instance, what do you do if you want to
be local? In these kinds of situations, and in the

very short term, I can understand that the incorporation strategy might be considered necessary. However, I do think that we should aim to avoid, and even dismantle, these situations where only hubris and a flight forward into concentration may appear 'reasonable'.

> In the secession scenario, would cities
> disappear or are they a crucial part
> of the scenario?

I would imagine them to be much less important. Cities are traditionally places of exchange and market. If we want to relativize the importance of the market economy, we must also de-emphasize the role of cities. It's as simple as that. In my view, people should become less professional or, say, less specialized. People should do several things: be part-time gardeners or farmers, and part-time something else. It is important for the future of the planet that people become more self-sufficient than they are today. I don't have very good examples (except a few important ones, like the Zapatist Chiapas), but some elements of jurisprudence may be found in different historical eras, like the feudal system. Thanks to custom rights and commoning, communities were much more self-sufficient. Markets existed, surplus could be traded and it was possible to meet other people with particular specializations. But they wouldn't flock to those huge centres of commerce, crave for commodities and sell their workforce because they had no other way to survive. If you want to employ somebody, you need first to deprive this person of their basic means of self-sufficiency.

> Is that possible with the current world
> population?

It might be impossible, but it's nonetheless highly desirable. Let me frame your question the other way round. When you look at the past, let's say at least the two to five last centuries in Western Europe, but in many other world regions as well, you cannot avoid the feeling that the urbanization of humankind is the sense of history. (Today more than 50% of the global population lives in what is described as urban concentration.) On the other hand, when you probe the future, especially with the environmental issues in mind, you cannot avoid the feeling that this continuous progression of the world's urbanization is the end of history. So we are confronted with a situation, a progression of the urbanization of the world, which looks both inevitable, and impossible.

To put it differently, I don't think that everybody can become autonomous all of a sudden, but I do think that any politics that doesn't have as its ultimate goal to make people less dependent instead of more is futile. How do we reverse the process of accumulation of capital that deprived people of their means of taking care of themselves? How do we give back those means, or at least help them to develop these means to take care of themselves, not as individuals, but as communities?

The more I think about these things, the more I tend towards Marxism. Even though Marx did not know anything about the actual biodiversity collapse and climate change, he provided a very good description of the logic behind the environmental issues as manifestations of the consequences of the accumulation of capital. I think Marx was right to say that the origin of these issues is not just the Industrial Revolution. It goes back at least to the fifteenth and sixteenth centuries, the famous Renaissance, that wonderful period of urban tropism, so dear to architects who consider it as the origin of their specialized discipline. One of the important things that Marx explains in the first volume of *Capital* is what he calls 'the law of accumulation of capital'. Accumulation can be understood here as growth. The law can be summarized as follows: the more growth there is, the more the value tends to be concentrated in what Marx calls 'the fixed capital', the means of production, the buildings, the things owned by fewer and fewer people, and it tends to go less towards 'the living or variable capital', which are workers, skills, etc. Of course, both fixed and living capital grow, but proportionally there is a kind of increasing discrepancy between these two.

In his last chapter he asks himself, How did that start? How was there a kind of first or initial accumulation that allowed this process to develop? Hence 'primitive accumulation'. It happened in the first place through colonization, meaning you just take everything: workers, resources, etc. Think of coffee, sugar cane, tobacco produced in mono-culture plantations, with an enslaved workforce. Simultaneously, in the countries where the accu-mulation started, this brought about the start of the dispossession of farmers. The enclosures of the commons meant that a large number of people didn't have sufficient means of production to sur-vive, so they had to leave the countryside, many of them becoming vagrants. Laws against vagrancy subsequently forced them to sell the only thing they had, which was their labour force, leading to proletarization.

> We were looking for arguments against
> the different scenarios regarding
> living together. What dangers or pitfalls
> do you see for the secession scenario?

Obviously, one of the major concerns is peace and security, ways of avoiding or taming the *Homo Lupus Homini* logic (man is a wolf to another man), the wills and struggles of power that might threat-en a federation of communities aiming at greater autonomy and self-sufficiency and engaging local-ly in a process of degrowth or de-accumulation. Such communities could be an easy prey for those (either states, corporations, gangs or pure surviv-alists) who are determined to pursue accumulation and predation to the ultimate limit. Medieval literature (the *Roman de Renart*, for instance) and the multiple threats, which the Zapatist organization is currently facing are quite instructive on these issues. But again, secession is less an ideal state than a process that has to progressively develop and adapt its own wisdoms so as to address and prevent these pitfalls. In my view, brandishing these threats as scarecrows to demonstrate that there can be no alternative to the pursuit of concentration, social control, and voluntary servitude, is a much more dangerous plea for irresponsibility.

> This idea of dispossession of farms is actually also a danger we consider in the infiltration scenario with urban agriculture as bottom-up initiatives and commoning practices. In the Netherlands there is the example of the Herenboeren project: 100 people contributing monthly in order to hire a professional farmer to produce food for and with them. In this way the farmer becomes actually a service provider with a salary. It looks good, but there is the risk that the farmer won't have a sustainable relation to the land, which is necessary in order to work within an ecosystem.

Yes, certainly. But it is not easy to go back to a situation where people had at their disposal the first element of the means of production, which is the soil. I'm also not saying that the feudal system was a good system, but as Marx says: we should be a little more attentive to what was interesting in that precapitalistic period, especially the system of common lands or even private land cultivated in common, benefitting from the tools of the richest labourers. The owners of a parcel had a right to the harvest on their parcel, but that was all. For the rest of the year, the cattle from the community could access the land. Property meant a stack of custom rights that has nothing to do with what was invented with the enclosures: exclusive property. Today an owner has, so to speak, every right on that land, and can eliminate any competitor, human and nonhuman, for the means of production. To answer your question, you need to have a stable relationship with your land, but exclusive property is not the condition of that stability. We have to find other ways of living with the land, and the case you mention, good or bad, is an example of (or a first step into) the actual quest for these other ways.

Nowadays there is also this question of how to deal with negative commons: things that we share and that are a burden, for example many industrial practices are destroying the soil in the countryside. In the scenario of infiltration, is there a new role for agriculture or cultivators to transform that toxicity and pollution?

Yes, certainly. An infiltration scenario is the penetration of agricultural or horticultural practices within the fabric of existing cities, in territories deprived of agriculture. It is the way agricultural uses in the wide sense of the term, like forms of commoning, are coming back. In this scenario, as in the others, reclaiming the earth from machines, chemical fertilizers, etc, and patiently rebuilding fertile soils on polluted grounds, should be considered a *sine qua non*.

What about depopulated mountains? In what scenario would you say Inland fits, the collective project started by artist Fernando García-Dory in Spain? It consists among others of a Shepherd School, an artist residency programme and a shop (online and in Madrid), where products are sold. What is intriguing about their way of working is that they use the art system to give value to local agricultural practices by actively participating in them.

The scenarios focus on the relationship between city and countryside. So in what we call infiltration, it's rather about things coming from the countryside and the field of agricultural innovation permeating the city, while integration is the other way round: it is the city extending and including agriculture within their programme. Because of the leverage of art, Inland resonates with the scenario of infiltration. Art is kind of urban. It is a form of accumulation. It is a form of professionalization. I think Inland is also a significant attempt to question this status. I am actually a militant of taking art from artists, to have that very beautiful word 'art' available again to describe very old and new practices like agriculture, for instance. For me, a good farmer today is the true artist: an athlete in the art of hoping.

> In our opinion, negotiation or integration is really the attitude most taught in architecture schools. It is also what we found in Flanders, France and Switzerland. It is complete control of what the farmer does. Since you also work in an architecture school, what do you think?

Some people think that you have to make the inevitable possible. If cities are still expanding, we have to change them, by integrating agriculture and forestry into their programme. It is the smoother version of the incorporation scenario. It is also a way of saving urbanism, because the more cities grow, the more they can build. No cities mean fewer architects. But we have to be cautious. What I often see is greenwashing. In France there is, for instance, this law of 'Zéro Artificialisation Nette':

the goal is to not encroach anymore on agricultural lands or on lands that could be cultivated. If you want to fight that law, integration is great: it remains agricultural land, but you can urbanize it at the same time. Please show me this is possible!

> Are we to understand that you don't believe in urbanism anymore, or at least that it should become less important? How do you think the work of urbanists should evolve?

Urbanism is quite a recent discipline. It appeared in the mid-nineteenth century, and only became common in the early twentieth century. It does not mean the creation of cities but the way of dealing with the considerable extension of existing cities. That happened because of the rural exodus and the growth of the population in general, stimulated by accumulation. Since I think that the extension of cities should stop, urbanism can only exist as a kind of medicine within the existing urban places. Twenty years ago I wrote that our problem is no longer the extension of cities, but the deepening of territories, especially the territories of agriculture, because most of them are monocultural deserts. We have to make them blossom, but not by planting cities on them. We should turn to permaculture, for instance, which is a kind of volumetric agriculture that can feed a lot of people. This would mean a drastic transformation and repopulation of the countryside, and a voluntary change in the politics of access to land. In a wonderful manifesto published a couple of years ago, the Atelier Paysan in France advocated the necessity of a million new farmers in France in the coming years (knowing that they are not even half that number today).

> In Flanders, where the agricultural
> policy is very much like the integration
> scenario, the state is funding farmers
> to plant extra trees and hedges.
> Everything a farmer does is highly
> controlled by the government. It is this
> idea of deepening the territory but
> from a top-down planning perspective.

The problem is that the city still has the whip hand and the farmer is a kind of employee, a service provider in the ecosystem services logic. We have to develop a macro-system, a type of agriculture that interacts with all other subjects: trees, shrubs, hedges... This idea of gardening a place will probably work in certain situations, it will sometimes even be necessary, because indeed cities are still growing, but I consider it still as medicine, a kind of last surgical operation of urbanism. It is not the cure.

I think permaculture or similar movements should supplant urbanism. They are a kind of urbanism in the best sense of the term, meaning a complex discipline linking all the elements of a place, except that in permaculture gardens or agroecology, most of them are living elements. You acclimate a place with plants and vegetables etc., it's a real sociology extended to non-humans. It's about making places resilient, it's about life. It's parametric, it is in fact a foil to urbanism. It's as complex, at least, as urbanism.

> Let's look at the notion of seasonality in the different scenarios. In the first scenario, a world where everything is controlled, seasons lose all links to the natural cycles of our environment and it becomes incorporated in the global market dynamics. How are we to think about seasonality outside of the productive cycles?

Seasons are not the same in cities as elsewhere. There, seasons don't mean a lot, except for tourism. Tourism is the incorporated way of inheriting seasonality in urban life. During working days you're in the city, and then during the holidays you leave and look for a place to soak up the sun. So we are all seasonal in a way, but not in a very interesting way.

> We thought about wwoofing (Worldwide Opportunities on Organic Farms): people interested in agriculture travel the world in order to volunteer on organic farms. They are often young people who live in urban environments and are looking for the experience of

living on a farm. It is a completely
different relation to work than a migrant
labourer who works in industrial
agriculture.

Wwoofing is indeed an interesting phenomenon
because it is quite widespread: a lot of people are
involved in this and for many it is the only good
or available way to get in touch with what it means
to cultivate a place. It has something to do with
secession.

Wwoofers are also seasonal migrants of a kind: at
a certain period in their lives, they try this out. But
there is at least an incentive to learn. Maybe they
just want to change their mindset, but it is coming
from them. If people at that age have a sufficient
degree of liberty and can afford that, I don't think
it's a waste of time.

> The seasonal workers we met also initia-
> lly did not consider seasonal jobs in
> Western industrial farms as their main
> occupation. They always started with
> the idea of quickly earning some extra
> money to build a house or start a com-
> pany in their home country. However,
> after some years many felt trapped,
> the seasonal activity becoming more and
> more dominant and they slowly lose
> the connection with their home country.
> Since they can't work in their own

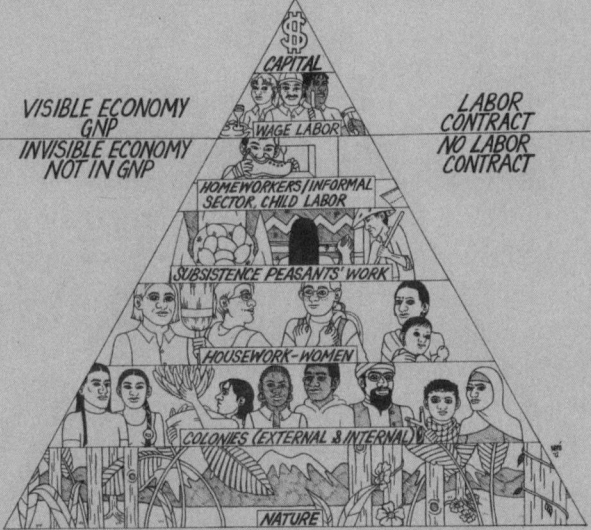

ICEBERG MODEL of CAPITALIST PATRIARCHAL ECONOMIES

CAPITAL

VISIBLE ECONOMY GNP — WAGE LABOR — LABOR CONTRACT

INVISIBLE ECONOMY NOT IN GNP — NO LABOR CONTRACT

HOMEWORKERS/INFORMAL SECTOR, CHILD LABOR

SUBSISTENCE PEASANTS' WORK

HOUSEWORK - WOMEN

COLONIES (EXTERNAL & INTERNAL)

NATURE

country during the period they work
in the West, the idea of collective autonomy or self-sufficiency is deferred.

Yes, it is under threat. I suppose they have to build
laws to limit the season, otherwise it becomes industrial exploitation. What if those people had a
minimum of their own means of production in the
places they come from? I don't know if they would
come.

We're not sure about that. We watched
Ceux qui Restent,[4] a film that tells
the story of the few people that decide
to stay in their village in Romania,
living from the land while most of their
neighbours travel to the West to earn
money, dreaming of a middle-class life-
style. It shows that in some ways they
could stay and take care of themselves,
because they have a place and access
to land. However, they do want more
comfort, which is understandable. It's
a question of what the person is looking for.

This relates to the work of Maria Mies, one of the
founders of ecofeminism. She came from a pre-war
village in Germany in the Eifel valley near Köln,
but worked a lot in India and became close to

4   *Ceux qui Restent*, a film by Anne Schiltz and Charlotte Grégoire, 2019.

Vandana Shiva with whom she published a book on ecofeminism. Together with two other feminist scholars, known as the school of Bielefeld, she developed the 'subsistence perspective', which basically argues that we should replace the logic of our current economy of accumulation by a logic of subsistence. Imagine a pyramid of society at the top of which you find the basic classes of society, first the capitalists and just below, the wage labourers. Marx dealt with that. But under these you have several layers without which the two on top wouldn't function at all: informal labour (the black market), peasants that take care of themselves and their children, phantom labour, often women taking care of what Marx called 'reproduction', and finally colonies and nature. The ecofeminist perspective is looking at those five invisible layers. How would you reorganize an economy from the perspective of subsistence? This doesn't mean they are advocating to render everything that is unpaid work paid. They are just saying that we have to recognize all these layers, and invent an economy whose centre of gravity would recognize the whole pyramid instead of focusing on the top. I'm actually doing a new section on this for the exhibition, because it's extremely relevant to our topic. In any case there is still a lot of research to be done.

Slash!

We slice pumpkins left and right as
our breath digs cavities into our chests.

Slash!

Eight hours lying face down on the
tractor-powered weeding bed.

Slash!

Agency reveals itself in the pumpkin
that accidentally a c c i d e n t a l l y
slips under the wheel.

Slash!

What space is there for negotiation
at the speed of efficiency and in
the absence of a shared language?

Slash!

There is nothing comfortable about it.

Slash!

BIOGRAPHIES

CLAIRE CHASSOT (FR/CH) works across performance, scenography and landscape design. She explores the gestures and movements that reveal the complexity of the relations between humans and plants. Seasonality and vegetal migrations underlie her research. She uses basketry and cartography as complementary tools to connect with specific territories. Often led collaboratively, her projects aim to reveal the tactile qualities of the landscape.

JONATHAN DE MAEYER (BE) holds a master's in visual arts and photography from LUCA School of Arts, Ghent. At the heart of his work lies the continuous development of a multidisciplinary image archive that forms the basis for associatively composed series and installations. Through the alternative and personal lens of his photographs, films and writings, his work aims to inspire new ways of perceiving and engaging with the spaces and landscapes around us. In addition to his autonomous practice, he likes to engage in collaborations with other artists and musicians.

ANASTASIA EGGERS (RU/DE) pursues a research-driven practice that explores vulnerable ecologies alongside urgent social, cultural and political conditions. She uses food as a medium to broach ideas of identity, origin and geopolitics. Eggers investigates agricultural rhythms that arise when our dependence on seasonal cycles is severed or when new dynamics surface due to geopolitical shifts or changes in market conditions. Her recent works explore rituals in agriculture as a tool to bring hidden narratives to light and to envision new forms of collectivity, coping and awareness.

CIEL GROMMEN (BE) extended her training in architecture at KU Leuven with a master's in contemporary art at HEAD in Geneva. The result is a collaborative trans-disciplinary research practice that engages with places shaped by a particular value framework. Producing temporary habitations, spatial installations, maps, events and stories, Grommen aims to invent new narratives of cohabitation, linking local perspectives to the global scale.

ILS HUYGENS (BE) is a curator, writer, editor and researcher. She has worked for almost fifteen years at Z33 House for Contemporary Art, Design and Architecture, curating exhibitions and projects in Milan, Rotterdam and Istanbul, among others. Her recent work has mainly focused on topics of global extraction and deep time. Today she is exploring the relations between contemporary art, ecology, climate change and the more-than-human. Besides the visual arts, she also works in film and is a co-founder of the cult-film festival Offscreen in Brussels.

PIA JACQUES (BE) is a graphic designer with a focus on the context and history of printed matter. Research is an essential part of her work, often departing from archival documents. Her practice takes multiple forms, including performance, writing and installation. She participated in the temporary master's 'F for Fact' at the Sandberg Institute, after obtaining her diploma in graphic design at Sint-Lukas Gent. In 2020 she co-founded the Belgian Institute of Graphic Design (BINGO), which researches and promotes graphic design in Belgium.

IOANA LUPASCU (RO) enjoys crafting experiences that encourage critical thinking and playful interaction, with a strong focus on process, making and methodology. As a host they facilitate spaces of learning and gathering that focus on collaborative productions of sound pieces, audio walks, texts, art installations, publications, poems, movement sessions and workshops, infused with elements of emergent play and storytelling. Ioana is currently drawn to exploring the themes of intimacy, residue, translation and fragmentation.

KAROLINA MICHALIK (PL/US) is a visual artist interested in exploring boundaries by subverting unwritten rules, unmasking and dismantling codes and hierarchies of modern society through visual and spatial embodiments. In her artistic practice she explores various sociocultural issues by immersing herself in a specific context and subsequently bringing her experiences and reflections together in words, images and sounds.

YACINTH POS (NL) is a designer and chef with a practice centred on the social, political and cultural field using a research-oriented approach. By exploring various mediums, she delves into social narratives, often focused on food and communal gatherings, where the methodology of design seeps into the construction of dishes. She investigates ways to enhance our awareness regarding food and crafts new dining experiences as a way to reflect on broader sociocultural issues. On a daily basis, you will find her strolling through nature, foraging wild edible plants and flowers.

CAROLINE PROFANTER (IT) is a composer and performer in the fields of electro-acoustic and acousmatic music. She works with field recordings, amplified objects, feedback systems and spatialized sound with the help of computer and analogue devices, collaborating frequently with other artists. Since 2017 she is co-artistic coordinator of the Q-O2 workspace for experimental music and sound art in Brussels.

MAXIMILIAAN ROYAKKERS (BE) interlaces artistic, pedagogical and architectural approaches in a transdisciplinary practice. In his work he engages with places and situations by setting up spatial practices that intertwine local perspectives with global dynamics, questioning social, political and ecological relations unfolding in space. He develops his practice by engaging with networks of local inhabitants, experts from different disciplines and collaborations with artists, architects and institutions. In doing so, he attempts to experiment with alternative ways of living together.

INES MARITA SCHÄRER (CH) works across poetry, performance, installation, sound art and experimental music. She is concerned with the precarities and vulnerabilities of diverse human and more-than-human beings in predominant power structures. She explores voice and words as a means of establishing relationality and of reimagining their conditions and environments. Her practice is informed by the given context, permeable to various forms of alternative knowledge forms, nourished and driven by thinkers, co-thinkers, collaborators and allies.

MONA THIJS (BE) writes, produces and directs stories. In her storytelling practice, she works with language in multiple ways and engages in conversation with people and places in order to find new narratives. Mona is currently developing her writing and production skills in the Slow Writing Lab. Together with Astrid De Haes, she is preparing *Blueberries Leave Bruises on the Skin*, a new dance/theatre production which will be touring in 2024.

EWOUD VERMOTE (BE) studied social sciences at Ghent University and audiovisual arts at LUCA School of Arts, Brussels. He currently teaches at Sint-Lukas secondary art school and is a member of PLAN B, a platform that supports artists from various disciplines in producing, presenting and reflecting on artistic practices based in a rural context.

CREDITS

COVER
Image by Jonathan De Maeyer
Drawing by Claire Chassot, Anastasia
Eggers and Maximiliaan Royakkers

THE ARTIST AS VISITOR
→ p. 22, 31: Images by Ode Windels
→ p. 19, 25: Images by Selma Gurbuz/Z33

CHANGING LANDSCAPES
→ p. 79 – 91: All images by Jonathan
De Maeyer

POST-SEASONAL RITUALS
→ p. 186: Illustration of *IJsheiligen,* Henri
Verstijnen, 1892 – 1940, Rijksmuseum,
Donated by Uitgeverij L.J. Veen
→ p. 186: Effigy of Morana (Death),
Czech Republic, Matěj Bařha,
Ethnographic Museum of the National
Museum, Prague, Czechia
→ p. 187: Sanctuary decorated for
Erntedankfest (harvest festival) in a
village church in Marbach, Willy
Hanisch, 1934, photo Marburg
→ p. 187: Germin: Harvest dance in
Schneverdingen, 1951, Deutsche
Fotothek
→ p. 188: Day of harvest and
collectivization (poster), Publishing
society "Bezbozhnik", Moscow, 1930,
Russian State Library
→ p. 188: France, Jura, Arbois, Place de
la Liberte, *Fete du Biou,* procession,
porters and grape cluster, Credit line
Hemis / Alamy Stock Photo
→ p. 189: Burning of the *Maslenitsa*
effigy, Apollinary Mikhaylovich
Vasnetsov, 1920, Moscow Regional
Museum of Folk Art Crafts
→ p. 189: Antique postcard with
depiction of *Les Brandons in Auvergne,*
France. https://www.regardset-
viedauvergne.fr/2012/03/fete-des-
brandons-en-auvergne.html

CHŁOPI
→ p. 207 – 219: All images by
Karolina Michalik

SEEDS AT THE TABLE
→ p. 226, 227, 232, 233: All images by
Ioana Lupascu

UNPACKING ROUTINES OF ARRIVAL
→ p. 248: Image 1: Empty *plukkaart,*
photo Carolien Lubberhuizen
Image 2 Sorting cherries at the end
of the day, photo made by Elżbieta*
Images 3 & 4: Feeling at home
in temporary spaces – photos made
by Marija* and Mirjana*
→ p. 251: Image 5: Enjoying the
sun – photo by Gabriel*

*pseudonyms of the workers

ATHLETES IN THE ART OF HOPING
→ p. 264, 268 – 270: All drawings
by Martin Etienne in discussion with
Sébastien Marot
→ p. 289: Hann Alexander Helios for
Ecosocialist Horizons

The two poems by Ioana Lupascu at
the start and end of the book are based
on the artistic research they did to
create the soundwalk *I am looking at
her looking at them looking at me.*

ACKNOWLEDGEMENTS

Aad, Paul and Rob van der Knaap from
Kwekerij PandA
Adinda Van Geystelen, Annelies Thoelen,
Jesse Bas and the whole team of Z33
Adrian, Anca, Cornea, Elena, Marek,
Patrick and Vasile
Adrien Balle from La Ferme du Grand
Lire
Afra, Bosco and Jon Rouvrois
Aisha, Melek, Ogi, Musti from
Momchilgrad
Alexandre Cudet from La Serre des
Marais
Ana Robles Pérez
Andżelika, Dorota, Gosia, and Tomek
Ángeles Morales and Manuel from
Eurosol Group
Anne Schiltz
Benjamin Mouly
Ben Neven and Chantal Timmermans
from Neven kleinfruit
Bidu, Gabi, Marco, Paula
Camille Gaillard and Salomon Tyler from
Collectif dallas
Bernke Klein Zandvoort
Charlotte Grégoire
Christiaan Feickens
Clemens Driessen
Daniel Balle
Edith Wouters from Ar-tur
Franky Vantyghem from Koekelare
Hedwig Ory
Hélène Balle
Hendrik Dupont and Hilke Neiss from
fruitbedrijf Neiss
Joost van Strien from Zonnegoed
Joséphine Tilloy
Kasia from farm Zonnegoed
Kasia Wlodarczyk
Klaas Burger
Kunstenplatform Plan B
Leen Delcroix and Steve Schrijvers from
Hoezaerenbosch
Lieve Apers-Mertens
Lukas from the Flevohoeve
Mihaela Lupascu
Milena Mulders from Migratie Museum
Nadine Vandromme

Ode Windels
Rawad Baaklini and Tiiu Meiner
Rebeca Ibáñez Martín
Špela Petrič
Theun Vandueren
Thomas Vaneste
Timothy Liu
Vanessa Brazeau
Vlad Ionescu

And all other workers, farmers,
community members and institutional
partners whose names are not mentioned
here but who inspired us with their
dreams and thoughts, and gave input and
feedback throughout our process.

COLOPHON

Seasonal Matters
Rural Relations

(Field)notes on rhythms, rituals and cohabitation

By Seasonal Neighbours

Onomatopee #252

Editors
Anastasia Eggers & Ils Huygens

Authors
Claire Chassot, Jonathan De Maeyer,
Anastasia Eggers, Ciel Grommen,
Pia Jacques, Carolien Lubberhuizen,
Ioana Lupascu, Karolina Michalik,
Yacinth Pos, Caroline Profanter,
Maximiliaan Royakkers, Ines Marita
Schärer, Mona Thijs, Ewoud Vermote

Proofreading
Patrick Lennon

Translations
Ils Huygens

Graphic Design
Bonsma & Reist

Publishing Year
2024

Publisher
Onomatopee Projects, Eindhoven (NL)
Jesse Muller & Natasha Rijkhoff

Printed by
Wilco Art Books, Amersfoort (NL)

Paper
Holmen Trnd 2.0, 70 gsm
Arena Rough White, 170 gsm

Typeface
Clarendon URW

This initiative was co-sponsored by the
Flemish Community and Grensverleggers
(scheme to support cultural collabora-
tions between parties in Flanders, the
Province of North Brabant, the Province of
Limburg and the Province of Zeeland).

Vlaanderen
verbeelding werkt

provincie limburg
gesubsidieerd door de Provincie Limburg

Provincie
Zeeland

Provincie Noord-Brabant

deBuren